Planted in Love

Published by Mark Gyde
First Published in Great Britain in 2014.

Cover design by Trevor Mason
Cover photograph © Mark Gyde

British Library Cataloguing in Publication Data
ISBN: 978-0-9567792-4-3

Planted in Love

What do our lives look like when we walk as Jesus walked?

"For this reason I kneel before the Father, from whom every family in heaven and on earth derives its name.

I pray that out of his glorious riches he may strengthen you with power through his Spirit in your inner being, so that Christ may dwell in your hearts through faith.

And I pray that you, being rooted and established in love, may have power, together with all the Lord's holy people, to grasp how wide and long and high and deep is the love of Christ, and to know this love that surpasses knowledge – that you may be filled to the measure of all the fullness of God."

(Ephesians 3:14-19 NIV)

Mark Gyde

To the Memory of John W Gyde
10th June 1934 to 18th October 1971
A true father, taken too early

To Fiona
My wife and best friend, who has shown me and our children what love is like.

Dedicated to my four children:
Frances, Hilary, Hannah and John
May your roots go deep in love as you walk as Jesus walked

I love you all.....

Contents

Foreword

In John 15:9 Jesus says, " *As the Father has loved me, so have I loved you. Now remain in my love*." The disciples understood exactly what Jesus meant when he talked about remaining in his love. They had walked with him for three years and had received his love and encouragement, his comfort and support. In being with Jesus they had learned to walk in daily dependence on the Father. Jesus had shown his disciples what a life of love was like and as he prepares them for his return to the Father, he encourages them to continue living in love. This too is his encouragement for us.

In this book Mark gives us some essential keys to help us remain in the Father's love. This is a book that is rich in biblical truth and revelation which Mark presents in an accessible and life-giving way.

Mark simply and carefully opens up the word of God and lays it out, line after line, like a rising tide of revelation. He is not afraid to address some contentious issues but does so by using biblical truth in order to win his readers over. This is a book that carries weight beyond its size. The depth of its insight and Christ-centred themes will delight our hearts and feed our minds.

I am sure you will enjoy reading this book.

Trevor Galpin – Fatherheart Ministries

Introduction

What does it look like when we live in love?

What is our life like when we live as a son or daughter? What will change as we grow in relationship with our Heavenly Father?

I believe that when we encounter the love of God, as Father, it is a life changing experience that will not, nor should not, leave us the same. In 1 John 2:6, John encourages us to walk as Jesus walked. This is not an instruction to draw up a list of all the things Jesus did and then try and imitate his miracles. It is an invitation to have the same lifestyle as Jesus had. Jesus' lifestyle was one of complete and total dependence on his Father. Walking as Jesus walked will lead us into that same lifestyle of dependence on our Heavenly Father.

If we want it, walking as Jesus walked will change every area of our lives.

Paul describes this transformation as being 'rooted and established in love' – or, **planted in love**.

Many of us may have had some experience of God as Father, but what happens next? How do we grow as a son or daughter to our Heavenly Father? How do we walk as Jesus walked?

Throughout this book I hope to answer these and other questions. I trust as you read, you will be drawn closer to your Heavenly Father and will discover that you really are planted in his love. It is only as we are planted in love that we begin to understand how vast and amazing this love really is.

Chapter 1

Living in love

"And so we know and rely on the love God has for us. God is love. Whoever lives in love lives in God, and God in him". (1 John 4:16)

Lamentations is not one of those books we read very often. Most of us know the few verses from the middle of chapter three which remind us that the steadfast love of the Lord never ceases and his mercies are new every morning. If we read those verses in context we see a picture of something that looks remarkably familiar. The writer is having a bad day. In fact, he may be having a bad month or even a bad year as everything is going wrong and he cannot seem to find any relief.

We feel the same when everything is going wrong for us: financially, health-wise, with our jobs, in our families, emotionally or just the constant struggle of trying to keep our heads above water. Sometimes these seasons seem to be endless and when we are in the middle of them, it is all too easy to lose sight of our Father and begin to doubt that he provides for us, that he cares for us or even that he loves us. The very real pressure of the things we face almost suffocates us and we are dragged away from living in the truth and experience of the Father's love.

In Lamentations 3:21-23, Jeremiah suddenly remembers something which once again brings him hope. He remembers that God's love never ceases and that his mercies never end. They are new every morning. He remembers that God is faithful. In the middle of his despondency he remembers that his Father is good and that he will not let him go. Even in the midst of pain and suffering there is hope.

We, too, can have hope. God is the same yesterday, today and forever and just as Jeremiah could remember and experience God's goodness, so too can we. Whatever our situation, we can call to mind the faithfulness, love and kindness of our Father. We can have hope. We can believe that, because of the Father's great love for us, we are able to be drawn back to the place of love. God does not stop loving us when we go through a hard or painful situation but sometimes we struggle to receive or live in the centre of his love for us.

I was talking with a friend who is working in Uganda and a few months ago she held a sick child who died in her arms. At that time she felt God had abandoned her; how could he love her if he could let this happen? As a result, part of her heart became closed to God and she doubted his love. Thankfully, that bit of her heart is being healed as she realises that God, her Father, was with her and was carrying her through that terrible experience.

Father wants to constantly remind us that his love is never ending. There is nothing that can take away his love for us, but sometimes we feel that the struggle of our everyday lives is overwhelming and we simply don't feel as if we are living in love.

If we read on in Lamentations 3 we see that Jeremiah, having remembered the faithful love of God, decides to wait quietly for the salvation of God. He sees the reality of his circumstances and faces them by drawing back into the reliable and life-giving love of God. This is an encouragement for us as we can face our circumstances in the same way, by drawing back into the love of our Father.

The reason we can do this is because the words used in 1 John 4:16 are experiential words. Knowing and relying on the love of God are not theological or theoretical concepts but they are words which mean we can stick to, recognise, touch and experience the love God has for us. These are words that belong in our hearts. They describe a relationship and a journey and in order for us to start this journey, we have to be prepared for our hearts to be transformed. Because we live in love we live in God and that gives us the assurance that his love (which is all of his character) is totally reliable and dependable. There is nothing about our Father which is unreliable. What we have to realise is that we are not depending on our own strength or personality but we are drawing life from the Giver of Life and it is this that leads us to the security and intimacy he offers.

John describes this relationship in his gospel (chapter 15) where we read that just as a branch of the vine is connected to the main vine, so we are connected to the Father, through Jesus. It is a relationship that is intimate, full of life and it is one which leads to the production of fruit. The fruit John talks about is fruit that will last and which will be abundant. This too, is the result of living in love. As we live in love and draw life from the Father our lives will be fruitful. All too often we do things that although good, are not ours to do and we wonder why we become worn out and tired. Jesus promised us a life of rest but this only comes when we are yoked to him in relationship and as The Message translation of the bible says, where we "walk with him, work with him and learn the unforced rhythms of grace". As we live this life we discover the truth of Jesus' promise. This is living in love. We become so connected to the Father that we start to live like Jesus, only doing the things which the Father is giving us to do.

What the does living in love look like?

Jesus spent the evening before his arrest with his disciples and during that time he prays some prayers which have eternal consequences. In John 17 he prays for himself, his disciples and for "all those who will believe in him" - that's us! In that prayer he says some things which most of us can hardly dare to believe despite reading them frequently. This is what he says:

> *I have made you known to them, and will continue to make you known in order that*

> *the love you have for me may be in them and that I myself may be in them. (John 17:26)*

Here he says that the Father loves each one of us with the same love and in the same way as he loves his son Jesus. In one sentence, Jesus has drawn us into the intimate relationship of the Trinity and invites us to realise that we are not second class citizens but that we are joint heirs with him. As Paul writes in Ephesians 2:6, we have been given joint seating with Christ in the Heavenly realms and so as far as he is concerned, we are with him. This removes all the performance and striving from our lives as we understand there is nothing more we have to do in order to be loved by the Father. Likewise there is nothing we can do which causes God to love us any less.

These are Jesus' last words before being led away to his trial and crucifixion and must therefore be important. They are the truth. We are loved as Jesus is loved and grasping the power of these words will change our lives. These words are not the reward for a full and busy life but are the true inheritance for everyone who has chosen to put their trust in Jesus and to believe that he is the way to the Father and therefore to life. If we can grasp the enormity of what Jesus is praying and truly believe that he has accomplished everything that needs to be accomplished then the door is easily opened for us to begin to live in love. It invites us to take a step of faith where we reach forward and take hold of the truth of his promise and draw it into the present reality of our lives. What Jesus said is a non-negotiable truth that many of us fail to grasp as we are overwhelmed by the pain in our hearts and the ingrained mindset that tells us we have to earn love.

At conferences and on Fatherheart schools I spend a lot of time telling people they can't earn love. We are loved already. This sounds simplistic, but all we need to do is fall back on the truth. You are a son. You are a daughter. The Father is already loving us. In fact he has always loved us and what we need is a divine revelation of this truth into our hearts. You don't have to be fully healed or to have dealt with all your stuff in order to live like this. In fact, the revelation of the truth will help you with your stuff and will facilitate your healing.

Another truth we receive by revelation is in verse 24 of the same chapter. We are with him. Jesus came from the bosom of the Father and that is where he returns to and in doing so he draws us into himself so we too are with him and the Father. Again, this is not a reward for living a good, productive life but it is part of our inheritance. The resurrection and ascension are not merely for his benefit; they are for ours well. Paul's letter to the Ephesians gives us greater insight into what Jesus is praying as he writes about our unity with Christ and our understanding of the magnitude of the Father's love for us. All too often we invite God down into our world so he can help us with our stuff and, in one sense, there is nothing wrong with that as he loves to help with the things that matter in our lives. But there is a greater destiny for us as sons and daughters.

He sees us seated in Heavenly places in Christ Jesus and he invites us to live in his world where we can experience the covenantal relationship of the Trinity. This is a relationship of freedom in which we are not only free from our sin, but also free from the striving that has held us captive. We are free to enter our rest and to begin to enjoy the unmerited favour of his grace showered upon us.

Knowing we are loved as Jesus is loved and beginning to enjoy the closeness of his presence leads to one other thing starting to happen. We become united with each other. 1 John 4:12 tells us that if we love one another then God abides in us and his love is perfected in us. As we love one another his love is made complete. This does not mean that if we choose to love others then God will choose to love us and live with us - that would make the Father's love conditional, which of course it is not. What it means is that when we live in love then the automatic outcome will be the overflow of his love from us to those around us. We do not seek love in order that we may give it away but as we receive love into our hearts it changes us so much that it expresses itself through us as the natural overflow of the life we have received. We are loved because we are loved. Receiving love is not a tool to equip us to live a better life but it is the very substance of who God is being made known to us. We can only ever love because he first loved us. This is the completion or fulfillment of his love.

As we live in love we are made complete (1 John 4:17). This is what we desperately need; not just so the wounds of our heart may be healed, not so we can forgive and release those who have hurt us but that we may live the complete and whole life which the Father designed for us. As The Message says: *"this way love has the run of the house, becomes at home and mature in us, so we're free of worry on judgement day - our standing in the world is identical with Christ's"*. This is a way of life which is rooted in relationship with the Father where we are free from striving and performance.

Completeness is us being restored to the Maker's original plan. God only has a 'plan A' and his desire is that we should be brought back to our true identity as his sons and daughters who, being made in his image, can live as Jesus lived. Wholeness is far more than having our emotional wounds healed, it is us being able to fulfil our true destiny.

The opposite of love is fear. As we live in love fear has to go. There is simply no place to experience fear when our heart is filled with love. The more we live in love the more fear has to go, they just can't exist together. Oh that this would happen instantly, but the reality is that we are in a process through which our hearts are changed as they are filled with love. As the transformation of love takes place so fear is driven out and we gradually begin to trust and depend on our Father more. Our lives become built upon a foundation of love and the reality and experience of 'knowing' and 'relying' on his love start to change us as we become rooted and grounded in love.

Living in love takes us on a journey where we seek relationship rather than religion, we learn to receive rather than achieve and we succeed through rest rather than the works of our own hands.

There are a few keys which will help us live and grow in love.

In Exodus 33 Moses basically cries out to God for help: "who is coming with me to help me lead these people?". He knows his own inadequacies and he asks God to teach him his ways in order that he might know that God's favour is with him. God's reply shows a true father's heart. He does not give Moses a rule book or a list of things which need to be done. He simply replies that his presence will go with Moses. That was true for Moses and it is true for each one of us. The first key to living in love is to know that the Father's presence is with us. We are not abandoned nor left alone. We don't have to fight unaided but we have his presence with us. In fact, in Deuteronomy 1:30-31 we see that he will fight for us, he will lead us and his desire is to carry us as a father carries his son ALL the way through life's journey. The first key on this journey is to realise that he has done it all. There is nothing we need to do so we can fall back into his open, waiting arms where we can be safe and where we can trust him with a childlike simplicity and dependency.

Secondly, we need to appreciate that our heart is slower than our mind. Romans 10:10 tells us that it is with our hearts that we believe. Our mind has the amazing capacity to process a lot of information very quickly. We are able to multitask. Whilst we are doing one thing, our mind can be thinking a thousand thoughts: what are we doing next, what are we going to say, how will we respond to what we have just heard? The trouble is all too often we live according to our mind and try to keep up with the vast amount of data it is processing and all that does is wear us out. The heart operates at a slower pace and living in love requires us to slow down and live at its pace. Slowing down may mean learning to say that little word 'no' and this may cause other people to have a problem. It is important not to become caught up with things, however well intentioned, which we need not be concerned with.

Thirdly we need to spend time with Father. Soaking, simply being with him or maybe just doing something you enjoy for relaxation can be ways of having time to listen to his voice and to be refreshed. A simple prayer you can pray at any time of the day (or night) is: "Father, fill me with your love right now". That's a prayer he loves to answer.

I'm sure there are many more things I could add but importantly we need the same heart and attitude as the writer of Lamentations who wrote: *"The LORD is good to those whose hope is in him, to the one who seeks him; it is good to wait quietly for the salvation of the LORD"* (Lamentations 3:25-26). His encouragement to us is to hope, seek and wait and as we do we will discover the faithful and unchanging love of the Father. We too can experience his mercies being new every morning.

I believe it really is possible to live in love. This does not result from following a formula but it comes out of relationship which is something that needs time to grow. Living in love takes a step of faith to really believe the truth of who we are, of who the Father says we are. Thankfully, there is someone who comes to help us and that is the Holy Spirit.

Chapter 2

The Holy Spirit of Sonship

"For those whom he foreknew he also predestined to be conformed to the image of his Son, in order that he might be the firstborn among many brothers." (Romans 8:29)

When I was a teenager our church experienced a wonderful and lasting move of the Spirit. This was in the 1970's during the charismatic renewal which was sweeping the UK and many other countries at that time. We enjoyed a wave of the Holy Spirit which lasted many years and completely transformed the life of our church. You never quite knew what would happen at the next meeting as there was an excitement and expectancy as we waited for the Holy Spirit to lead the meetings.

My mother and her friends were very much part of this but, at the time, I was a bit on the sideline for some very good reasons (or so I thought). I was in my last year at boarding school and certainly did not want to go back to school having been baptised in the Holy Spirit. So I made a deal with God, which I have since discovered is never a wise thing to do. I agreed that if he would leave me alone, I would be baptised in the Spirit when I left school. The only problem with that agreement was God never signed up to it – it was simply me telling him what I thought he should do.

A year before I left school we were on a national church camp (the Dales Bible week in Harrogate). One afternoon our church had its own meeting during which there was a word of knowledge for someone who needed to be baptised in the Holy Spirit. Well, it was a word of 'knowledge' alright! Everyone knew I was the only person lacking in this area. I managed to resist the endless encouragement and went away relieved that God seemed to be keeping his side of the bargain. But as I said, making a deal with God is never a wise idea and during the Christmas holidays that year, I finally succumbed when a good friend offered to pray for me to receive the Holy Spirit.

Shortly after leaving school, I got the results of my final school exams which were not good enough to enable me to go to university so I started training to be an accountant at a firm in Oxford.

I also became very immersed in the life of the church. There was a young couple who had recently moved into the village and were part of the church. At that time Roger was a pig farmer and we loved listening to his stories of daily life in the pigpen. He always seemed to be able to hear what God was saying and brought the church many words of encouragement. Roger taught me how to listen to Father's voice, he taught me to move and grow in the gifts of the Spirit and he passed on his enthusiasm for the things of God. Many years later we led the church together in our town of Abingdon.

1994 saw the outpouring of the Father's blessing which began in Toronto and then spread across the world having an impact on many churches and the lives of many individuals. We had weekly 'River of God' meetings where, once again, we experienced the excitement and expectancy which comes from the unpredictability of the Holy Spirit. This season lasted for several years and was a period of refreshing for many of us.

For the church, one of the hallmarks of the late 19th Century and 20th Century was the reawakening of desire for a Spirit led life. The Welsh revival, the Hebridean revival, Azusa Street and the Pentecostal and Charismatic renewals all served to refresh the church with the life and power of the Holy Spirit. What began in small pockets has spread through every denomination and sphere of Christianity so that the Holy Spirit is now welcomed and has become a real part of church life. As prophesied in the Scriptures we see and experience the signs and wonders that follow and accompany any move of the Spirit. I regularly listen to podcasts from Bethel church in Redding, California and hear stories of amazing healings and transformed lives. That church has a vision, not just for individual lives but for whole communities and cities to be transformed by the power of the Spirit and the love of God.

I don't intend to do an in depth study of church history, others have done that in more detail and much more skilfully than I ever could. Suffice it to say the church has enjoyed 150 years of a renewing and reawakening brought about by the presence of the Holy Spirit. This has built on the revelation of Jesus as Saviour which Martin Luther introduced us to through the Reformation.

So we have a church which is comfortable with the gifts of the Spirit and which is starting to see the fruit of the Spirit manifest amongst its members. Maybe we are starting to live what Watchman Nee describes as the normal Christian life.

But I believe there is much more for us to see and experience about the life and work of the Holy Spirit.

I wonder how much the disciples were aware of as Jesus approached the end of his life. I guess they sensed something was about to happen when Jesus explained he was leaving them and returning to his Father. But I imagine they had no idea of how events would unfold and how they would be feeling. As they ate their last meal together they probably felt uncertain of what was happening as they tried to grasp what Jesus was talking about.

In John's gospel, we are given the clearest account of the mealtime conversation during which Jesus takes time to carefully explain all that is going on. He explains that his leaving is not the end but the beginning of something new through which the Father will be revealed in a greater way.

Jesus tells us that he is going back to his Father in order to prepare a place for us (John 14:1-3). Whilst we use these verses as a source of comfort at funerals they have a much greater significance for us. Jesus promised to make a home for us to enjoy, not just in the distant future but for us to live in NOW. Where he goes, we go. Where he is, we are. We are with him right now and, John tells us, that place is right at the Father's side or right at the very heart of the Father (John 1:18).

You can imagine the disciples' confusion when Jesus said these words. Thankfully, Thomas put into words what they were all thinking: 'What are you talking about, we haven't a clue where you're going, tell us and show us the way' (my paraphrase). Jesus goes onto explain that he is the Way and, as Derek Prince said[1], 'a way only has meaning if it leads to a destination. Jesus is the way, but the Father is the destination'.

If I'd been one of those disciples I think I'd be getting more confused by the minute. What on earth is going on?

In three short verses Jesus sums up exactly what is happening. He sees the confusion and apprehension of the disciples and because of his love for them, he explains what is going to happen through his death and resurrection. He knows that during his time with them, he has been like a father to them. He has led them, he has taught them, he has comforted them but above all he has shown the power of a life lived in love. He has been a living example of the transforming power of love. As he loved his disciples they have changed from a disparate band of rough and ready men to a family who would shortly change the face of religion for ever. Jesus is the perfect representation of the Father and so, in his relationship with the disciples, he had been the Father to them. Just as God the Father is love, so Jesus is love.

Jesus fully appreciates the disciples' concern that they are about to be left fatherless, or become like orphans. And so in John 14:16-18 Jesus tells them, and us, what is going on:

> *"And I will ask the Father, and he will give you another Counselor to help you and be with you forever – the Spirit of truth. The world cannot accept him, because it neither sees him nor knows him. But you know him, for he lives with you and will be in you. I will not leave you as orphans; I will come to you."*

The Holy Spirit is God on earth[2], he is God's own Spirit who has been given to us. Not just given to us but given to live in us, to guide us into all truth and to communicate and impart the Father's love into our own hearts (John 16:12-15). The Father's Spirit lives in us to father us so we know that we are no longer orphans. If we are not orphans we have to be sons and daughters. The Holy Spirit connects us in relationship to the Father.

In Galatians 4 Paul re-emphasises this. We are not slaves or orphans but we are sons and daughters. Because we are sons and daughters God has taken his own Spirit and put him into our hearts so that we are able to cry out 'Abba, Father'. 'God you really are my Father'. Something happens deep within us when we receive the Holy Spirit which removes the emptiness and loneliness of our hearts and brings us into a revelation of who God really is and who we really are. We are not orphans, we are sons and daughters. As Jesus said in John 8:35 we belong! Because we belong we are free, we are no longer held captive by the power of religion. Instead we are caught up in the eternal relationship of the Trinity.

In Romans 8 Paul re-visits this theme once again. We are not controlled by our sinful nature but we are controlled, or motivated, by the Spirit of the Father who is living in our hearts (Romans 8:9). The Spirit in us gives us life and we know the life Jesus promised was an abundant one. For too long we have allowed the enemy to steal that life away from us, that's what he is good at – Jesus said the thief comes to steal, kill and destroy but **he** gives us life (John 10:10). Because we have this life within us we have, as Paul says, the Spirit of sonship by which we can cry out 'Abba, Father'. 'God you really are my Father'.

The Holy Spirit connects us in relationship to the Father.

For a moment let us look back at the Old Testament. There are several passages in which the prophets look forward to a time when God will change the people's hard hearts of stone into hearts of flesh. This speaks prophetically of what Jesus won for us on the cross.

Ezekiel 36 probably puts this most clearly:

> *"And I will give you a new heart, and a new spirit I will put within you. And I will remove the heart of stone from your flesh and give you a heart of flesh. And I will put my Spirit within you, and* ***cause*** *you to walk in my statutes and be careful to obey my rules. You shall dwell in the land that I gave to your fathers, and you shall be my people, and I will be your God." (Ezekiel 36:26-28 ESV)*

When the Holy Spirit comes and lives in us, we are given a new heart and a new spirit which will **cause** us to walk in the Father's ways. Something inside of us is transformed so that we become motivated to do will of the Father. The very core of who we are is changed by this Spirit of sonship. Does this sound familiar? This was how Jesus lived. The desire of his heart was to please his Father and to walk in his ways. As we walk in the Spirit and allow his life to rule our hearts we will see a growth and multiplication of the fruit of the Spirit in our lives and this begins with the fruit of love. Such a transformation is only brought about by the Spirit living in us and not through our own effort or desire to live a good moral life.

As we read about the Holy Spirit I wonder if you begin to see him in a different light?

We desperately need the gifts of the Spirit which are described in 1 Corinthians 12 and Romans 12. We desperately need to see more of the fruit of the Spirit written about by Paul in Galatians 5. We need to experience the joy that the Holy Spirit brings. C S Lewis wrote[3] that 'joy is the serious business of Heaven', he really had grasped something! We need a greater experience of the joy of the Lord amongst us.

If we look at the Holy Spirit as a tool box which is filled with good things, that we can dip into and pull something out to help us, then we are missing the point. The gifts of the Holy Spirit, which have been so much part of the charismatic renewal, are vital to the life and health of the church but they do not define the totality of the Holy Spirit's role in our life.

Jesus put it so well in John 14. The Holy Spirit is the Spirit of the Father who lives in us so we can know without a shadow of doubt that we have a Father. The Holy Spirit is the spirit of sonship that sets our hearts free to be alive and then this new life erupts out of us crying 'Abba, Father'. 'God you really are my Father'. The Holy Spirit connects us in relationship to the Father.

The illustration I often use is that of a bridge. I will ask a couple of people (often a husband and wife) to join me at the front, standing a couple of metres apart with me in the middle. One of them represents the Father and the other is us. I play the part of the Holy Spirit and take their hands forming that link between the two. That is what the Holy Spirit does – he connects us to the Father. But it is more than that. I describe the Holy Spirit as an elastic bridge that draws the Father and us close together, in fact we are drawn so close that we become one.

This is the picture Jesus paints for us in John 14. The Holy Spirit coming to reveal the Father, to live in us and to draw us into the centre of the Father's heart. The Trinity has chosen to make their home in our hearts (John 14:23).

When the church in Toronto experienced the wave of the Spirit in 1994 they called it the Father's blessing. John and Carol Arnott were very clear, this was the Father pouring his love into our orphaned hearts in order that relationship could be restored between us and our Heavenly Father. I believe the Arnotts caught hold of something – the Holy Spirit is a Spirit of love who longs for our hearts to be connected to the Father's heart. I wonder if we should re-define baptism in the Spirit to being baptised with the Father's love into sonship.

The Holy Spirit is the Holy Spirit of sonship. He draws us into relationship with the Father and our hearts become free. We start to realise that our freedom is like a two-sided coin; we are free **from** our past life of sin and we are free **to be** sons and daughters. Our destiny is to live as the Father's sons and daughters in exactly the same way as Jesus did. He lived his life in obedience to his Father. It was not the result of slavish duty but came straight from a heart which desired to please. The freedom the Holy Spirit brings turns us around so we too can live from desire and not duty.

Relationship is not about collecting facts or information it is about life. There are two occasions in John's gospel where Jesus encourages us to drink living water and thus to partake of life. Just as a magnet attracts certain metals so a son is attracted to a father. But turn the magnet round and it repels the thing it is trying to catch. That's the heart of an orphan - it repels, or pushes life away, rather than being attracted to it.

The Holy Spirit of sonship enables us to know the Father. In Matthew 11:27-30 Jesus says *'no one knows the Father except the Son and anyone to whom the Son chooses to reveal him'*. Jesus is in the business of revealing the Father, it's what he loves to do. As we see the Father and know what he is like we finally find the way of rest. We learn the unforced rhythms of grace as we discover that he does not lay anything heavy or ill fitting on us (The Message).

When the Holy Spirit lives in us we live in relationship. As Jesus reveals the Father so the Holy Spirit living in us transforms our hearts with love. God has put his Spirit in us and therefore we inherit his character and personality. We become like Jesus (Romans 8:28-29). We are being transformed into his likeness from one degree of glory to another (2 Corinthians 3:18).

An encounter with the Holy Spirit needs to take us beyond the excitement of the encounter, it needs to take us beyond a desire for the gifts. It needs to take us to the place where our heart is changed by love. Having written in detail about the gifts of the Spirit Paul ends 1 Corinthians 12 by saying 'now I will show you the most excellent way' – the way of love.

As we live in love we will be changed, we will become like Jesus. We will start to live in our true identity which is described for us in Ephesians 3:14-21:

> *"For this reason I kneel before the Father, from whom every family in heaven and on earth derives its name. I pray that out of his glorious riches he may strengthen you with power through his Spirit in your inner being, so that Christ may dwell in your hearts through faith. And I pray that you, being rooted and established in love, may have power, together with all the Lord's holy people, to grasp how wide and long and high and deep is the love of Christ, and to know this love that surpasses knowledge—that you may be filled to the measure of all the fullness of God. Now to him who is able to do immeasurably more than all we ask or imagine, according to his power that is at work within us, to him be glory in the church and in Christ Jesus throughout all generations, for ever and ever! Amen."*

We belong to a family which is named after our Father in Heaven. He has unlimited resources which go beyond our wildest dreams. He will strengthen us and give us the power of the Holy Spirit. He will cause us to be planted in love to such an extent that we begin to grasp how huge his love really is.

The Holy Spirit is given to make this a reality, he comes to connect us in relationship to our Father.

AND BECAUSE YOU ARE SONS, GOD HAS SENT THE SPIRIT OF HIS SON INTO OUR HEARTS, CRYING, "ABBA! FATHER!" SO YOU ARE NO LONGER A SLAVE, BUT A SON, AND IF A SON, THEN AN HEIR THROUGH GOD. (Galatians 4:6-7 ESV)

NOTES:

1. Derek Prince Teaching Letter no 17 – "To Please My Father"
2. Taken from a podcast by Bill Johnson, Bethel Church, Redding, California
3. Letters to Malcolm: Chiefly on Prayer

Chapter 3

An Open Heart

"...that the God of our Lord Jesus Christ, the Father of glory, may give you the Spirit of wisdom and of revelation in the knowledge of him, having the eyes of your hearts enlightened, that you may know what is the hope to which he has called you, what are the riches of his glorious inheritance in the saints" (Ephesians 1:17-18)

As we saw in the previous chapter the Father has chosen to make his home in our heart. It is into our heart that the love of God is poured through the Holy Spirit. Just as a home can have areas that people are not allowed to go into, so our heart can have parts which we keep tightly locked and buried away from everyone. Our heart is very sensitive, fragile and easily wounded. It is either because of the wounds or pain we have suffered or because of the fear of more pain that we shut off areas of our heart. We do it for self protection and self preservation.

The Holy Spirit is not a bully nor does he want to be an unwelcome guest. He only goes where he is invited. If part of our heart is closed he will not force his way in, but he gently woos us and invites us to open that part of our heart in order that it may healed and filled with love.

The heart is central to all that we are. This is why we take a lot of time on our Fatherheart Ministries schools to talk about the heart and the ways in which blockages can be removed in order that the love of God can fill it. Two of the major blockages we spend a lot of time on are unforgiveness and regaining the heart of sonship. It is not about flicking a switch to make God love us, that is already the case. Right now he is loving you completely and unconditionally. He has always loved you. It is about clearing the stuff out of our heart so it can become a container for his love which then enables us to experience and live in his unconditional love.

In John 4, when Jesus talked to the Samaritan women at the well he offered her something which he also offers to all of us. He offers us living water that will satisfy the very depths of our being; he offers us life. He is not talking about changing the external things of our life but he is addressing the very core of who we are. He is talking to our heart so that it may be set free from everything that holds it captive.

Jesus did not come to give us an ideology or a set of principles but he came to introduce us to his Father. He came in order that we might be set free from religion and legalism and that we might have an intimate relationship with him and his Father.

When Jesus was tempted in the wilderness Satan tried to destroy his heart. He challenged and tried to undermine the relationship Jesus had with his Father.

Jesus, on the other hand, always appealed to people's hearts and spoke life into them.

It is very easy to read a number of Bible passages and arrive at the conclusion that our hearts are bad and that there is no hope for us: Jeremiah 17:9 'the heart is deceitful above all', Ezekiel 11:19 'I will remove from them their heart of stone', Matthew 12:34 'how can you who are evil say anything good? For out of the overflow of the heart the mouth speaks'. This is not particularly good news and if we are honest, we recognise that these verses describe the state of our heart.

But if Jesus is calling us to intimacy with him he must know something about the state of our heart that we don't know. He gives us hope. Hope that our heart can change.

We therefore need a transformation.

King David knew this. Out of his brokenness and weakness he cries out to God for a new and undivided heart.

> *"Teach me your way, O Lord, that I may walk in your truth; unite my heart to fear your name." Psalm 86:11*

David wanted his heart to change so he could understand and follow God's ways. He wanted a heart that could be filled with love and a heart that could have the brokenness and pain healed. He wanted a heart that was pure.

> *"Create in me a clean heart, O God, and renew a right spirit within me. Cast me not away from your presence, and take not your Holy Spirit from me. Restore to me the joy of your salvation, and uphold me with a willing spirit." Psalm 51:10-12*

King David is described as a man after God's own heart. We do not know all that David had gone through as a young boy but it is clear that he suffered a lot of rejection. When Samuel came to anoint one of Jesse's sons, David was not included but was left outside looking after the sheep. In Psalm 27 he writes of his mother and father forsaking him. When he took food to his brothers, who were in the army trying to fight Goliath and the Philistines, they rejected him and tried to send him back home to look after the sheep.

Despite all this rejection, when David is anointed by Samuel we read that the Holy Spirit 'rushed on him from that day forward' (1 Samuel 16:10-13). There was something about his heart which pleased God.

When we look closely at David's life we can see what it was that pleased God. He had something Saul lacked and that was the heart of a son. After killing Goliath he was adopted into Saul's family and treated like a son. Even although there was intense jealousy on Saul's part he treated David as part of the family. There must have been something attractive about David that drew him into the king's family.

Even after being taken into the king's household we read that David went back home regularly to see his father and to look after the sheep. David's brothers left the family home to follow Saul but David kept returning home. He had no fear when he played music before the king in his demented and tormented state of mind. When he had the opportunity to kill Saul he refused to, but instead cut the corner of his robe to let the king know he had been there. In fact, the next day he cries out to Saul 'See, *my father*, see the corner of your robe in my hand' Even as Saul tries to kill him he recognises what Saul is to him and seeks to honour him with his heart.

Despite all the rejection which David had experienced he was able to maintain an open heart towards those who would continue to reject him or try to harm him. He had the heart of a son.

The story of the two lost sons in Luke 15 describes two different hearts. Both of which were closed, not only to their father but also to each other. They did not want relationship with their father and had totally closed their hearts so that he had no place in their lives. One took his inheritance and went and lived a selfish, sinful life. As we know he eventually came to his senses and returned home, not as a son but as someone seeking the place of a servant. The other had closed his heart so much that he could not have any relationship with his father despite living in the same house. In his heart he felt like he'd been slaving away for no reward (despite him too having received his share of the inheritance).

Both of these sons had closed their heart and as a consequence were unable to enjoy relationship with their father.

In whatever ways we have closed our heart there will always be a loss of relationship. It may be that we have closed our heart to our parents, to our brothers or sisters, to our husband or wife or to our colleagues or friends. As our heart is closed so we distance ourselves and something of those relationships is lost. I realise that we close our heart to protect it but in doing so it becomes closed to those people and in some way closed to our Heavenly Father.

The way we relate to our parents colours the way we relate to God. The way our parents treated us affects how we think God will treat us. That's why dealing with these hindrances is a big factor in us being able to open our heart to the Father. That's why we have to go through the pain of opening our heart and letting the love of the Father heal and take us deeper into relationship with him. He loves to heal our hearts but he does so in order that we might be able to enjoy the greater reward of living as sons and daughters. He is jealous for all of our heart.

Make no mistake there is a battle for our heart. Just as Satan attacked Jesus' heart so he attacks ours. He is a thief with one intent and that is to kill and destroy everything that Father is doing in us. He does not want us to enjoy relationship with Father, nor does he want us to walk as Jesus walked. He does not want us live in the centre of the Father's heart knowing that we are the beloved.

But he is a loser.

There is a battle, but we are on the winning side. Jesus has paid the full price in order that we can enjoy our full inheritance as sons and daughters and also that we can live loved.

The heart is central to this battle which is why Solomon writes: *"Above all else, guard your heart, for everything you do flows from it."* (Proverbs 4:23). The truth is we have been given a new heart, a heart of flesh, but it still needs to be protected and guarded carefully.

The way we experience everything is conditioned by the state of our heart. As our heart changes we will automatically be transformed.

One of the privileges of ministering the love of the Father is to see people choose to open their heart in order to embrace their true identity as the Father's son or daughter. For many this is a painful process which may take months or even years to go through fully. But as they choose to forgive, as they choose to recover the heart of sonship they begin to experience the truth which is that they are loved in exactly the same way as

Jesus is loved, they **are** sons and daughters. This is the truth and it is always wonderful to see people begin to believe it as they allow the transforming power of love to work in their heart. For some it takes great courage to let go of the past and to go through the pain in order to live in the glorious freedom of the sons of God. But as they open their heart they receive something which makes it all worthwhile.

I add a word of caution here. To open a heart which has been deeply wounded means you have be able to trust. You need to be in a safe environment where you know you can trust those who are seeking to help you. If you do not trust, there is the fear of further abuse or pain and that is not a healthy situation in which to receive healing. If you do not feel safe then it may be better to wait rather than opening yourself for more wounding or pain.

Not only do we need to trust but we also need to be able to take a step of faith. It is Father who heals and restores. He is the perfect and complete expression of love. He is always good. As we open our heart we are responding to the voice of love which comes straight from his heart to ours. It is the voice that woos us deeper into relationship and it requires that step of faith to put our little hand into his big hand and to become totally dependent on him. As Jack Winter used to say: 'can you be a little boy or girl who needs to be loved?'

Our heart needs to be open if we are to live in love. When our heart is closed we have erected barriers which prevent the love of God being fully manifest in our lives. A closed heart is one that is locked and shuts out people and the redemptive work of love. This is very different to the careful stewarding of our heart which we read about in Proverbs. When we guard our heart we protect it from abuse or attack, we defend it against the lies and theft of the enemy and we carefully protect the fragile life of love which is growing within us. When you have young plants, you nurture and care for them so they can become strong and are able to stand against the storms of life. You keep them in a safe place until they are strong enough to be planted on their own in the garden. So it is with our heart. We protect it while it grows but we ensure we feed it what it needs. A closed heart is unprotected and unfed.

Sometimes there are big blockages we need to remove but other times there can be little things which happen and cause our heart to close down for maybe just a short period. When we live in love it becomes a habit to keep our heart open and to prevent anything taking hold of it which could become a stumbling block. As we walk as Jesus walked we forgive and go on forgiving, we receive love and go on receiving love, we are comforted and go on receiving comfort and we open our heart and seek to keep it open. (We will look at walking as Jesus walked in a later chapter.)

In Ephesians 1:17-18 Paul prays that the eyes of our heart may be opened in order that we *"may know what is the hope to which he has called you, what are the riches of his glorious inheritance in the saints".* Opening our heart, and seeking to keep it open, is a foundational step to being able to live in love and being able to walk through a doorway into freedom and into our glorious inheritance. An open heart is the container for his love.

"AND HOPE DOES NOT PUT US TO SHAME, BECAUSE GOD'S LOVE HAS BEEN POURED OUT INTO OUR HEARTS THROUGH THE HOLY SPIRIT, WHO HAS BEEN GIVEN TO US."

(Romans 5:5)

Chapter 4

Dealing With The Older Brother

"My son, the father said, you are always with me, and everything I have is yours." (Luke 15:31)

The story of the two lost sons is probably one of best known stories told by Jesus. Basically one son wishes his father were dead as he demands his share of the estate and family property. If you look back to Deuteronomy 21:18-21 you will see that this son deserved to be hauled before the elders of the city and then stoned for his rebellion and hard-heartedness. The father in the story does not do that but instead he divides his property and gives it to **both** of his sons. The younger son had no relationship with his father. He did not want to live under the covering of love nor did he want to belong to that family anymore. His heart was closed.

The older son was not much different. Whilst he did not ask for his inheritance it is clear that he had also closed his heart to his father. In his heart he feels like a slave, always having to work hard to please his father. Actually he does not see him as a father but as a master.

As we know from the story the younger son has a change of heart. He decides to return home. He recognises that his father's servants are treated better than he'd been whilst feeding pigs and so, not believing in any chance of redemption, he decides to offer himself as a servant. The father will have none of it; as far as he is concerned once a son, always a son. Before any questions are asked or any stories heard he re-instates his son into the family and gives him back everything he had left behind.

The older son could not cope with that. His response is poisonous: 'I've served you, I've never disobeyed you, you never gave me a goat, but for this son of ***yours*** you have killed the fattened calf". There is no desire for reconciliation on his part.

There is something in us which loves being the younger son. We recognise our own stupidity in choosing to walk away from the Father's house and trying our luck at being independent. We recognise our failings and shortcomings and of course we love the welcome we receive when we return home.

We often say it is a good job the younger son was not met by his brother. We point the finger at the church and declare it full of older brothers but, if we are the church, surely we are pointing the finger at ourselves. That is the truth. The older brother is in all of us. The older son represents us all – it is not good enough to point the finger of blame at everyone else. We need to look into our heart and see that the same attitudes and thoughts are lodged there just as they were in the older son.

When we live in love the older son has no place in our hearts. It is the transforming power of love that will drive him away and change our hard stony heart into the true heart of a son or daughter.

The older son's first response when his brother returned home, was "I've always served you'. He, no doubt, had watched his brother dishonour the father, take the inheritance and then go and squander it. One brother seems to be having the time of his life whilst the other is being a good dutiful son and continuing his faithful work on the family farm. His service did not come from a heart of sonship but from a slavish duty where he thought he was doing the right thing. How many of us live our Christian lives like that? We do the right things, we work hard, we lose our joy but we continue to believe that we are living a good moral life.

That's not what Jesus offered. He came to give us life and life to the full. Not a life that leads to us being worn out and tired by our religious duty. God does not want slaves, he wants sons and daughters. When we live our lives consumed by slavish duty all we can do is point people to a master. When we live as a son or daughter we introduce them to a father, our Father.

The second accusation he made was 'I've never disobeyed you'. The Father is not primarily after our obedience, he is after our hearts. He seeks relationship first and foremost. In Psalm 40 we read that God does not desire sacrifice and offerings but he longs for people to have an ear to hear his voice and a heart that desires to do his will. Three times in John 14 Jesus tells us that love comes first and from it flows obedience.

The Passion Translation puts it like this: *"Loving me empowers you to obey my word"*.

Too often we get it the wrong way round. We believe our obedience will earn his approval and as we earn his approval so we will feel loved. That view has tainted the church's thinking and teaching for centuries. It makes Father's love conditional on our behaviour. It is quite simply the wrong view. We are loved because we are loved. We are loved because God is love. We can only love God if we have first received his love (1 John 4:19) and the more we live in this extravagant and overwhelming love the more we will love. As we grow in love, obedience becomes more natural as there is a longing in our heart to do his will. Without that longing obedience is the response of a slave to a master.

The third response of the older son was 'you've never given me anything'. At the start of the story we read that the father had realised his estate and had given it to **both** of his sons. The eldest son would have inherited twice as much as his brother but it is clear that he had not been able to receive it in his heart. He carried on being a slave whereas he was really the owner.

We have received an amazing inheritance. The Father sees us as joint heirs with Jesus and seated with him in the Heavenly places. He promises to be a Father **to us**. Not just to **be** our father, but to actually father us every day of our lives. As his children, we have no need to be anxious about our lives or to worry about the things we need. We can place our trust and reliance in him, believing he will provide 'more than we ask or think'. He is a good Father and he delights in lavishing his love on us simply because we are his children.

To live like the older brother, where we can't or don't receive our inheritance, is to settle for a life of poverty. I am not talking about material things but the state of our heart. We have been offered abundant life, but we choose to remain poor when we continue living in our independent ways. Our hearts become bankrupt if we try to live out of our own strength.

Finally, the older son reveals his true heart. 'This worthless son of **yours** has squandered his inheritance on prostitutes'. Firstly, he cannot even accept that this is his brother. He has not been with his father, watching and waiting for his brother to come home. There is no pleasure or joy for him at this family reunion. There is nothing in his heart which shows any compassion towards his brother as he returns home. All he shows is bitterness. And secondly, how does he know that his brother has squandered his money on prostitutes? All we are told about the younger son is that he spent the money on reckless living. That could mean anything, but the older son makes the assumption and then accuses his brother in front of the rest of the father's household.

Let's not point the finger at others; let's have a good look at our own heart. How often do we assume and then accuse. We put two and two together and it's not four that we get! We look at what other people are doing, how they spend their time or their money, we look at their possessions, the house they live in or the car they drive and then what do we do? We make judgements and criticise. We leap to conclusions based on knowing part (or none) of the story and then we accuse.

What do our accusations do? They keep us away from others and keep us outside of the Father's house. We don't lose our salvation, nor does Father reject us, but instead of living in the centre of his presence we move into the outer courtyard. This causes our heart to be closed and when the Father comes to invite us in all we can do is respond with the same venom as the older son.

When we accuse and condemn others we have a similar heart response to the older son. We don't recognise other people as part of the family. We stop treating them like brothers and sisters and they become strangers, people with whom we have no desire to be acquainted. We lose sight of the family that we are a part of as we continue to live outside the Father's house.

What about some other responses which are hinted at in the story?

There is a lot of pride in the older son's heart. He considers himself to have higher and better standards than his brother. After all, he has done everything he thought was expected of him. He would never do what his brother has done, he would not dishonour his father in such a public and humiliating way. What he fails to realise is that his proud attitude has caused just as much, if not more, separation from his father. In Isaiah 14 it was pride which caused Satan to claim that he was like God. Pride always causes a breakdown of relationship and as we see in this story, it seems that it is harder to overcome. The younger son could acknowledge his sinful and rebellious way of life but the older son seems unable to do the same with his proud and arrogant attitude thinking he is better than his brother.

When we are bitter or resentful towards others we are being like the older son. Holding things against people is not the response of an open heart but comes from a heart with walls built around it. Jack Winter said that bitterness is like a poison pill we swallow hoping it will kill the other person. The only one who really suffers from our bitterness is us. It may hurt other people but it will eat us up from the inside.

When we compete with other people we are being like the older son. What we are really doing is seeking to push others down in order that we become seen and so people take notice of us and praise us for our good works. In the story of Cain and Abel, shortly after Abel has been killed God comes to Cain and asks where his brother is. Of course, God knows exactly where Abel is and he knows what has happened to him. His question to Cain 'where is Abel your brother?' is greeted with the same poisonous response as the Father gets from the older son in Luke 15. 'I don't know, am I my brother's keeper?'. He took no responsibility for his brother and there was certainly no love lost between them. God never asks a question without knowing the answer and the implication of his question was 'of course you are your brother's keeper'. That's what family is all about. We are to look out for one another and encourage one another. We are to care for each other and to prefer others above ourselves. We don't need to push ourselves up and makes ourselves look good. We don't need to stamp on others in order to be noticed.

How do we feel when other people we know are praised? Jealous maybe. Why do we feel like that? Barry Adams, John MacDonald and I do a live webcast on Wednesday evenings and the people who join us have the opportunity to post comments into the chat area. At the end of the talks there is usually a lot of encouragement for the speaker. Just occasionally, I find myself looking at all the positive comments which are said about Barry or John (and of course they are all true) and a thought goes through my mind 'nobody says that about me'. Instead of thinking that this is something we do together and when one of us is praised we all are, there is a twinge of jealously. Why? Because there is something in us that wants to be seen and recognised. There is a hole in us that needs affirmation.

Both sons had closed their hearts and therefore something inside of them had died. When our heart is closed there is something dead inside of us which is why the father said of the younger son *'this brother of yours was dead, and is alive again'*. As his heart changed something inside him came alive once more. That's how it is for us; when we open a closed heart something inside us comes alive. Through this well known story Jesus offers us the chance to change and to, in effect, undergo heart surgery. We are invited to see ourselves as one of these sons and we are invited to change our closed heart in order that it can become alive as it is filled with love.

We have no indication from the story whether the older son ever had a change of heart or whether he was able to welcome his brother home. Maybe Jesus left the ending open so that his listeners could have the chance to look into their own hearts and see what they were really like. In leaving it open-ended Jesus leaves us, too, with the opportunity to look into our heart and to make that decision.

Have you ever asked yourself what should have happened in this story? If the older son had not been so focussed on his slavish duty then he would have acted very differently. When his brother left home I think he would have followed him and tried to bring him to his senses and then take him back home. Sadly his heart was so messed up that he couldn't do it.

Going after the younger son was what another older brother did. Our elder brother Jesus, left his home in order to pursue those who were lost and then bring them back to his Father. Jesus came after us and brings us back to the open, waiting arms of our Father. He did it for the younger son and he longs to do it for the older one as well.

We are the older son.

We cannot fall into the temptation of making everyone else the older son, that's too easy and it removes from us the need for change. In Matthew 18 Jesus encourages a heart transformation within each one of us that will enable us to enter his Kingdom. What we try and do is deal with the older son at an institutional or organisational level. The heart of the older son is only present in organisations because it lives in the people who make up those organisations. To deal with it, we first need to start with ourselves. We need to look at our own attitudes and ask the Father to fill us with his love in order that we become more like our older brother Jesus, and less like either of the sons in Luke 15.

Although it is our decision, it is not something we need to do in our own strength or on our own. By choosing, we take responsibility for our heart but we are then enabled by the life and power of the Holy Spirit in us. We have the true elder son ready, not only to show us the way to the Father, but also to become the way. He leads us to the place of reconciliation with Father where the empty orphan ways of our heart can be transformed by his love, so we too can leave our slavish duty behind and begin to live as sons and daughters.

The father reminds the older son that he has always been with him and that everything he has belongs to him. I don't know if the older son could receive that. Can we? Do we know we are always with him and that everything belonging to the Father is ours as well? As we deal with the older son in us we can start to know and believe the truth.

Yes, we are always with him and yes, all that he has is ours.

Chapter 5

Being Free From the Expectations of Others

There are many things which try to rob us of life and which can cause deadness to creep into our heart. If we are aware of these things then we can guard our heart against their effect. As we see things creeping up on us we can take action to prevent them overwhelming us or strangling the life which is growing in our heart.

One of the things that can rob us of life is other people's expectations, particularly in regard to how we live our Christian life. The thing is, their expectations may appear reasonable and may be presented as a means for us to grow spiritually. They might be good things which need to be done, but if they are what other people expect then they can suck life out of us. Expectations can be like a millstone around our neck particularly if the level of expectation increases once one target is met.

We're used to doing what we're told. From an early age we're taught to obey our parents; in school we have to do as the teachers say and then at work we have a boss. For some, the only brief period of time it seems we can do what we like is when we leave home and enjoy three years of student life: staying up all hours, wearing what we want and maybe doing the occasional bit of work to satisfy our tutor.

Very often we try to meet other people's expectations because we want to please them. We may want to make ourselves look good or try and win their favour or approval. Inside all of us there is a need for affirmation and we think by meeting the expectations of others we will find the satisfaction our heart craves. Our need for affirmation is only fully satisfied when we hear Father speak into our hearts and tell us that we are his beloved son or daughter. Our other achievements may be good but the satisfaction and pleasure we derive is short-lived and something inside of us needs more.

The search for affirmation I have just described seems very passive. Sadly there can be a more violent response where the wounds in our heart are so deep that we seek attention by being as angry, as violent, as drunk or abusive as possible. In our pain we are screaming for attention and for the love we may never have received.

In addition to us trying to meet other people's expectations there are occasions when they put their expectations on us. This can be subtle and manipulative but the effect is they begin to control us and our unique identity starts to be stolen away. I have met many people who have lived under this oppression without realizing that they are being subtly controlled. There is something appealing about being showered with warm praise, but when it is only given to manipulate or coerce then it is false praise and not from the heart of the Father. It is only as we step out of control that we see it for what it is and realise that we have lived a life trying to please others rather than seeking to please our Father.

The moment someone tells us what to do, or how to live, we stop living from our heart and enter a life of performance and striving where we constantly seek to achieve what is being placed on us. We end up wearing an ill fitting yoke which wears us down and robs us of the rest and peace Jesus promised. Instead of the Father's law being written on our hearts we start to live according to someone else's law.

When we live like this we lose something of the joy of relationship with the Father. Our faith almost becomes second hand as someone else stands between us and God and seeks to super-impose their standards or beliefs on our life and thereby change our relationship with Father.

There is a lot of freedom as we step out of this cycle of control and begin to live as Jesus lived. We listen to our Father's voice and ask him what he would have us do. The words of John 5:19 *"I tell you the truth, the Son can do nothing by himself; he can do only what he sees his Father doing, because whatever the Father does the Son also does"* become our words. This is not an excuse for independence or wilfully doing what you want, it is merely giving Father the rightful priority over and above the expectations of others.

What then is our response?

If it is wrong for people to tell us how to be a 'good' Christian is it ok for us to do what we 'feel' like doing? On one level that sounds alright as it ***could*** speak of a relationship from the heart. We may, however, want to bear in mind Judges 21:25 where it seems it was not a particularly good idea for everyone to do what was right in their own eyes. Proverbs 14:12 tells us that what seems right to a man may ultimately lead to death. I do not believe the opposite to a life of control or meeting other people's expectations is the freedom to do as we please. Neither of these alternatives will take us down the road to life.

The desire to do as we please can be the default way of thinking for many people, particularly for those who are young or immature in their faith. This thought pattern mirrors the post-modern world which has removed God, as a divine being, from our way of thinking. God, and therefore the definition of absolute truth, has ceased to exist and has been replaced by a subjective set of beliefs in which each individual is free to define his or her own way of life. Truth has ceased to be absolute and has become relative, changeable and undefined.

Defining truth outside of God leads to a very weak foundation. You only have to look at politicians' speeches over a period of time to see how truth changes like the shifting sand on a seashore. Truth is sadly defined by what is popular at any point in time.

But Jesus said he **is** the way, **the truth** and the life. The truth he was speaking about brings freedom as we become sons and daughters of the Father. Jesus does not show us one paradigm of truth, he personifies truth. Truth therefore ceases to be a concept or set of values and becomes a person. Truth is based on relationship and so interpreting truth outside of Jesus is relativism which is dangerous as it takes us away from the certainty of God's Word. Truth will always lead us to see who we really are. Jesus tells us that the truth (him) will set us fully and completely free and when we enter this freedom we realise we are no longer slaves but sons and daughters (John 8:31-38).

If we move away from the centrality of the truth found in Jesus we can allow our feelings and circumstances to dictate our interpretation of God's Word. Rather than bringing and submitting our lives to the plumb-line of God's Word, we bring them to the swinging pendulum of our desires and emotions.

Of course, there are many things I 'should' do: in the UK I should drive on the left, I should drive clockwise round a roundabout, I should not drink and drive. If I choose not to do these things I face a penalty for failing to keep the law. There are other things I should do as well: I should love my wife and children, I should care for them and provide for them, I should be courteous to my staff and clients. If I fail to do these things there is no penalty for breaking a law but there would, nonetheless, be a consequence and that can be damaged or broken relationships.

We have, therefore, to steer the right course between legalism and libertarianism. Neither is right and both will lead us away from the satisfying life we are promised.

People should not tell us how to live our Christian life, but neither are we necessarily free to do as we please. If we are to find a correct response and true guidance on how to live we need to see what Jesus said. Jesus goes beyond saying 'you ***should*** do this' but instead says 'you ***will*** do this'. Three times in John 14 (verses 15, 21 & 23) he tells us to obey his commandments, not as a request but as an instruction.

If we listen to these words in isolation we could become trapped in religious duty and obligation rather than entering into the freedom we are promised.

What Jesus actually says is: "**if you love me**, you will obey my commandments". True obedience flows from a heart of love. It is the direct consequence of being in love with Jesus. Obedience is not a legalistic requirement but an automatic response to the love of God being poured into our hearts. We wrongly see obedience as satisfying the law, but Jesus sees it as the only and obvious response to being in love.

Jesus develops this in John 15 as he talks about abiding in the vine. Love draws us into him. As we live in him our lives bear fruit and that fruit is the result of his words becoming our actions (verses 7-10). Yes, there is discipline (pruning and change) but rather than it being a punishment it is a means to greater fruit, life and freedom. Jesus' promise to us is that his joy will be in us and our joy will be made complete (verse 11). All the joy of Heaven (which is quite a lot!) is our reward. It is not the reward for slavish duty but is a consequence of living in love.

It has always been the Father's desire to write his law on our hearts (Jeremiah 31:33). When we live in love his word ceases to be the burden of the law but instead it becomes a source of life within us. We are led away from bondage into freedom and it becomes possible for us to be fruitful as his life flows through us. The Psalmist put it so well: "*but his delight is in the law of the Lord, and on his law he meditates both day and night. He is like a tree planted by streams of living water that yields its fruit in its season, and its leaf does not wither. In all that he does, he prospers*" (Psalm 1:2-3).

Many of us have grown up expecting God to punish us because we perceive his word to be a list of rules and regulations which we cannot possibly keep. We have cowered away from him in fear rather than being free to enjoy a full and fruitful relationship with him. Our concept of God has been radically incomplete as we see him like the older brother sees him; a master rather than a Father. We believe he is angry with us because we never seem able to achieve the high standards which we think he expects. We fail to realise that he has no expectations of us as he simply wants to enjoy us being part of his family. Sadly, the expectations which other people place on us have also drawn us away from the truth and we end up striving, not only to please God but other people as well. The weight of expectation bearing down on us suffocates the life within us and we become a hard working, yet joyless, group of people.

God's plans and purposes for us can only ever be good. He is the complete expression of love and is the same yesterday, today and forever. He does not want us to suffer under the weight of expectation but longs for us to shake it off and enter the freedom which comes out a relationship with him. I encourage you to take a few moments to examine your way of life. Are you doing things in the vain hope of trying to please God or win his favour? Do you think that by pleasing others you will be a better person? The point is, everything that needed doing has been done. Jesus has done it all. There is nothing we can do which will win his favour, it is already won. We can freely enter and live in his presence because all the barriers have been torn down through the work of Jesus on the cross.

When we live in love, with his law written on our hearts, obedience loses any sense of duty or heaviness and it becomes a desire. Sacrifice and obligation are taken away and replaced with a listening ear where we are attentive to the loving voice of our Father (Psalm 40:6-8). We 'do', not because we 'should', but because we love. In fact, when we have his Spirit (the Spirit of love) within us we will be compelled or caused to walk in his ways and to obey his laws (Ezekiel 36:26-27). Love will be the force that motivates us and leads us to a way of living where the heavy yoke is removed from our shoulders.

As we live in love it is not an excuse to do as we please nor is it an opportunity to stop doing the things we may have been doing. It is an opportunity to pause and to consider what the Father would have us do. It is a chance to let go of duty and obligation and replace them with relationship and desire. Jeremiah 6:16 suggests we stop at the crossroads and ask where the good way is and then choose it, in order that we may find rest for our souls. Letting go of those expectations requires us to stop and consider what is really important before changing course and pursuing life.

> *This is what the Lord says: 'Stand at the crossroads and look; ask for the ancient paths, ask where the good way is, and walk in it, and you will find rest for your souls. But you said, "We will not walk in it." (Jeremiah 6:16)*

As we can see not everyone is prepared to make that choice. Rather than choosing the path of life, some prefer to carry on as before and therefore miss out on the life of rest and peace which is on offer.

We always have a choice. God will never impose his will on us; yes, he wants us to obey his word but he will not force it on us. If God imposed his will on us that would result in us being controlled and manipulated and love would cease to exist. True love gives us the choice to decide that **we want to**, rather than we have to.

In the Bible, there are many things that we are encouraged to do. At different times or seasons in our life some may be more relevant or important than others. However, the issue is not should we do them, but rather what is our motivation for wanting to do them. Equally there are things we should not do as our Father knows they are not good for us. The choice is ours, but we have a tutor who steers us towards the right path and seeks to prevent us from wandering off into our own folly. Titus 2:11-14 reminds us of the power of grace working in our lives. We are told that the grace of God has appeared: to bring salvation, to teach us to say 'no' to ungodliness and worldly passions, to help us live self controlled and godly lives and to be a people who delight in his ways and enjoy doing his work. God's grace is like a set of railway tracks as it keeps us going in the right direction in the security of his plans and purposes.

Ultimately it is not our words that communicate the most, but it is the life within us. If we say we have measles but actually have chicken pox, then it is chicken pox that people catch from us! People need to see us living in the Father and delighting in doing his will, rather than hearing our opinion of what they should or should not do. If we are delighting in doing his will, because of his love in our hearts, it will be infectious. We need to be free from other people's expectations but we also need to ensure that we do not put our expectations onto others. The moment we do that we put them under a law, our law! As we seek our freedom we need to find ways of releasing others into their freedom so the very thing we wish to avoid is not something we put onto others.

Our goal should be *"that Christ may dwell in your hearts through faith—that you, being rooted and grounded in love, may have strength to comprehend with all the saints what is the breadth and length and height and depth, and to know the love of Christ that surpasses knowledge, that you may be filled with all the fullness of God'*. (Ephesians 3:17-19 ESV)

Truth leads to freedom. True freedom is having a heart of sonship where we have an overwhelming desire to please our Father and to do his will. His commands are not burdensome but are the doorway to relationship and fruitfulness (1 John 5:1-5). As we abide in him we **will** know the truth and it will set us free to live in the Father's house as a son or daughter for ever. (John 8:31-38)

NOW A SLAVE HAS NO PERMANENT PLACE IN THE FAMILY, BUT A SON BELONGS TO IT FOREVER. SO IF THE SON SETS YOU FREE, YOU WILL BE FREE INDEED. (John 8:35-36)

Chapter 6

The Real Reality

"On that day you will realise that I am in my Father, and you are in me, and I am in you." (John 14:20)

It seems that whenever you turn on the TV, whichever channel you look at, all you seem to see are 'reality' shows. Saturday evenings can be spent channel hopping where you can be mesmerised by celebrities dancing on ice or wooden dance floors, young people trying to impress the judges with their singing, celebrities having thousands of insects poured over their heads or talent shows which are more about embarrassing people than entertainment or talent. And if that is not enough, Sunday evening has the results show (which was probably recorded after the live show on Saturday evening). In case you need more – Monday to Thursday evenings you can have the gossip of what is happening backstage, how the rehearsals are going and details of where you can buy the t-shirt, mug or calendar.

Basically we are being conned. 'Reality TV' is as far from reality as the east is from the west. We are being manipulated to have a desire for things we can never obtain. We are shown a lifestyle that is made attractive but is never going to be the substance of our everyday lives. The unreal is dressed up and sold to us as if it is real. We know in our heart of hearts that this lifestyle is fictitious, but we are led to believe we can reach for something that is beyond us as we witness this 'perfection' being portrayed on our TV screens. Quite simply, 'reality TV' is unreality!

It's not just TV shows that serve up a concentrated diet of unreality. Banks offer us loans to buy things we can't afford, cosmetic companies tell us their products will make us stunningly beautiful and eternally young and every supermarket tells us their products are the most healthy and the best for a balanced diet. We feast on this unreality but the yearning of our hearts is not satisfied.

What does all this have to do with living in love I hear you say?

The point is we are all seeking something. We want to find what the **real** reality is, what is the substance that will fill our hearts and finally satisfy the hunger deep within us? If we feed on unreality we always want more of the same but it leaves us, well – wanting more of the same. There is a need in our hearts for truth, for the **real** reality. If we don't find the truth then we will continually pursue things which only satisfy for a moment but do not deal with the deeper issues of our heart. When we are fully satisfied our hearts come to a place of rest and peace where the striving and struggle of our internal motor is halted.

In this chapter I want to highlight two realities and hopefully show you which is the real one for us to receive as we learn to rest in him.

The first reality is that of our daily lives where we are faced with routine things like going to work, doing the cleaning and cooking, caring for the family, facing the the financial challenges of making ends meet; in fact, all of the pleasures and hassles we face every day. These things are important and they consume a huge amount of energy and resources. I guess most people want to do their best at work, to be able to please the boss, to see promotion and an improved standard of living for them and their families. We all want to enjoy our recreational pursuits and have more time away from the office so we can enjoy our hobbies, families and friends.

There is nothing intrinsically wrong with these things. We need hobbies. We need recreation. We need these activities to give our mind a rest and to refresh our soul. Engaging in recreational activities is one way for our body to be restored and rested after all the busy things we have to do. We need to have a job and to see fulfilment from what we achieve.

This is the reality of our everyday lives. These are the things we have to consider and apply ourselves to on a daily basis. They occupy a lot of our time and hopefully we are able to enjoy some of the reward they bring.

For us, what we do between getting up in the morning and going to bed at night is to us reality.

But there is a danger. However good all these activities are there is the possibility that they will consume us and take us over. This happens when we think we are defined by our work, our family, our hobbies or even our church life. If our identity becomes inter-twined with our activity we can fall into the trap of being driven and the focus on our everyday reality overtakes us.

It is easy for us to define reality as the things we are involved in and which take up all our time. I do not diminish these things, they are necessary and important but we need to guard against them becoming the main focus of our life.

There is another reality that is sometimes less easy to see. This reality is the way the Father sees us and I would go so far as saying that it is the **real** reality.

The way Father sees us is very different to the way we see ourselves. He sees our true identity and destiny and draws us into it at every opportunity. We get bogged down in the frustrating stuff of our everyday lives, we see and feel our own inadequacies, we see and experience relational breakdowns and trauma. He sees us as the beloved, as his sons and daughters, as joint heirs with his son, Jesus. He knows only too well the frustrations we feel, but he is not limited in looking at the external things as he sees (and knows) that he has chosen to make his home in our hearts.

Paul understood what this was all about and he gives us a glimpse of it in many of his letters. He understood something Jesus said to his disciples shortly before he was taken away to his death:

> *"On that day you will realise that I am in my Father, and you are in me, and I am in you." (John 14:20)*

At the beginning of John 14 Philip makes a statement I guess many of us make. 'Show us the Father and that will be enough'. In that one sentence Philip has captured the cry of our hearts – Show us the Father! I always feel a bit sorry for Philip as Jesus seems to rebuke him for blurting out his heart's desire. Without that statement from Philip, we may not have had the following verses which show us the truth of our relationship with Father and the basis of his ongoing love being poured into hearts.

Jesus' reply is profound. Basically he says that we are caught up and included in the wonderful relationship of the Trinity and so far as the Father is concerned, we are in Christ. We are not kept at a distance, but the Father himself has chosen to make his home in our hearts. Where he is, we are.

He gives us his Spirit, he takes away the orphan emptiness of our hearts and he gives us one of the most amazing presents ever. His Presence. He sees us as he sees Jesus.

At the end of John 17 Jesus concludes his earthly ministry with these words:

> *"I have made you known to them, and will continue to make you known in order that the love you have for me may be in them and that I myself may be in them." (John 17:26)*

As we live in love we are drawn into him so we can experience and enjoy a unity with him and become a demonstration of his love to this hurting world. This is how the Father sees us.

In Romans 8 Paul writes that there is no condemnation for those who are in Christ. This does not mean we suddenly stop sinning and live a perfect life. It does not mean we use 'grace' as an excuse to do what we like on the basis that we are already forgiven. No, it means that when the Father looks at us he sees the perfect work of Christ being manifest in our lives. The work of the cross does not give us a licence to do what we please but it covers the mistakes we make so the Father sees us covered with the redeeming blood of his son. Grace, Paul tells Titus, is to teach us to say 'no' to ungodliness and worldly passions and to enable us to live a God-centred and love filled life (Titus 2:12-14).

Living in love is discovering a grace filled life that is focussed on living like, and becoming like, Jesus. It's a life where we choose to delight in doing his will and letting obedience become a pleasure rather than living by a set of rules that are impossible to keep. This is how the Father sees us.

One of the common phrases throughout Paul's letters is 'in Christ'. He has fully grasped the truth of what Jesus was saying in John 14.

As we read Ephesians 1:3-2:10 we see our true inheritance and the blessings that are ours in and through Christ:

- We are blessed with ***every*** spiritual blessing in Christ
- We are chosen in him
- We have been made holy and blameless in his sight
- We were predestined to be his sons and daughters
- He has freely given us grace
- We have been redeemed
- Our sins have been forgiven
- He has shown us the secrets of his heart (the plans he brought into existence through Christ)
- We are chosen
- We are made alive in Christ
- We are seated in Heavenly places with him

When I read this list I ask myself 'is that a reality in my life?' That is how the Father sees me but is it how I see myself? It is easy to let circumstances dictate what we believe about ourselves but here, in Ephesians, Paul holds a mirror before us so we can see ourselves as Father sees us. He presents us with the truth to show us that we are one with Christ and that we have direct access to the Father (Ephesians 2:18). We are not foreigners or aliens but we belong to the Father's household and are part of his family. This is how the Father sees us.

Bill Johnson once said that any revelation of God will always lead to us having a greater intimacy of relationship with him. He is Father. He is love. As we discover the truth of who God is we can't help but be drawn into a closer relationship with him. In Colossians 2:2 Paul prays that we may be encouraged in heart and united in love in order that we may have 'complete understanding'. Complete understanding of who we are in Christ. Later in the chapter Paul tells us that **all** the fullness of the Godhead dwells in Christ **and** that, as we are in him, this full life extends to us. Amazing as it sounds we are filled with the fullness of the Trinity. This is not something we earn through hard work, but it is a gift given to us through our baptism and resurrection into new life.

Paul's famous prayer in Ephesians 3 gives us a glorious picture of the enormity of the Father's love and it ends with him praying that we would be 'filled to the measure of all the fullness of God'. (Ephesians 3:19). This is how the Father sees us.

In Colossians 2:17 we read that reality is found in Christ. There are many things that can drag us away or pull us down but the truth is found in our relationship with the Father. Outside of Christ we become governed by rules and regulations that wear us down and steal our life. Jesus came to show us the truth which is that our lives are hidden with Christ, in God. Jesus showed us what a relationship with God looked like, it is a son walking and working with a Father. This is what our life can look like as well, we are sons and daughters walking and working with the Father.

> *Since, then, you have been raised with Christ, set your hearts on things above, where Christ is, seated at the right hand of God. Set your minds on things above, not on earthly things. For you died, and your life is now hidden with Christ in God. When Christ, who is your life, appears, then you also will appear with him in glory. (Colossians 3:1-4)*

This is how the Father sees us.

When you travel on the London Underground, at several stations you are instructed to 'mind the gap' between the train and the platform. It is a bit like that for us as we try to cope with these two realities. There is a tension between what the Father sees and what we see and experience every day, where the usual ups and downs of life are mingled with the wounded state of our hearts. Living with this tension is part of living in a fallen world and it is easy for the immediateness of our lives to overwhelm us. All too often we become embroiled with the immediate and lose sight of what is really important. At work, when people are prioritising their time, I encourage them to consider what is important and then to focus on that rather than being diverted into the things which appear to be more pressing.

In highlighting the two realities we face, my encouragement is to turn our gaze onto the **real** reality so we begin to see ourselves as Father sees us. I understand that the circumstances of life often make this difficult as there are many things which demand our attention. Being planted in love helps us with this process as the more we are rooted and established in love the more we will see ourselves as God sees us.

As with 'reality TV', it is easy to be lulled into a false sense of security where we chase after something we think will satisfy, only to find that any pleasure is temporary. It is easy to give ourselves to our work, family, hobbies or church only to discover that there is still a hole in our heart. It is easy for the wounds in our heart to shout louder than the truth and so we settle for something less than we were made for. It is easy to let the reality of our everyday lives suffocate our true identity and destiny.

Father knows all about our lives. He is with us every moment of the day and he knows what we are going through. All the stuff of our lives does not deter him or catch him unawares. He knows, yet he sees us through his eyes and he sees the truth of who we are. He sees us as his sons and daughters. He believes in us. All those things we read from Ephesians are true and they are for us to begin to enjoy now.

In Matthew 18:3-4 Jesus encourages us to turn around, humble ourselves and become like little children. It is as we do this that we enter his Kingdom and experience the truth of our destiny as sons and daughters. We begin to experience the true reality which is our inheritance. Philip wanted to see the Father so he could enjoy the same relationship as Jesus. He knew there was something greater which he and the other disciples were missing; he longed for that intimacy with the Father. He voiced the cry of our hearts and the reply he received is the one we receive. It is possible to live in love, simply because the Father sees us in a way we do not (yet) see ourselves. The Father sees the truth of who we are and who he has made us to be. We are his sons and daughters. Our lives are hidden with Christ, in God. All that belongs to Jesus belongs to us. We are loved in exactly the same was that Jesus is loved. We are the beloved on whom his favour rests.

I know we find this hard to believe sometimes, but it is the truth, it is the **real** reality. This is how Father sees us.

Chapter 7

The Authority of Sons

> *"Let each of you look not only to his own interests, but also to the interests of others. Have this mind among yourselves, which is yours in Christ Jesus, who, though he was in the form of God, did not count equality with God a thing to be grasped, but made himself nothing, taking the form of a servant, being born in the likeness of men."*
> (Philippians 2:4-7 ESV)

In chapter 2 we looked at the Holy Spirit of Sonship who lives in us and enables us to cry 'Abba, Father, God you really are my Father'. It is the Holy Spirit that causes us to grow as sons and daughters and enables us to walk as Jesus walked. As you may have realised through reading the last few chapters there are blockages which the enemy uses to steal our life away and to prevent us from living in our true destiny.

As we live in love we can see those blockages being torn down and we begin to live in the real reality as we start to see ourselves as Father sees us. We are being conformed to the image of Jesus (Romans 8:29) and transformed from one degree of glory to another (2 Corinthians 3:18).

When the younger son comes back to the family farm (Luke 15) one of the things the father does is to put a ring on his finger. That ring signifies authority. Despite everything that has happened, and even before the son's story is heard, the father reinstates him in the family and gives back to him the authority he had walked away from. Once more the son could go into town and act on his father's behalf. In business, it was as if the father himself was there completing the transaction. The ring meant that people had to take notice of the son and listen to him as if they were listening to the father. Despite all his failings, the father sees him as a son and by giving him the ring, allows him to function fully as a son. No one would have had any doubt, this boy was back!

There is another occasion in Scripture when someone is given a ring of authority and that was after Joseph had interpreted Pharaoh's dreams and forecast the seven years of plenty being followed by a severe famine. Pharaoh recognises the authority with which Joseph speaks and places him in charge of the whole land of Egypt. He takes his ring off his finger and puts it on Joseph's finger, he then dresses him in fine robes and places a gold chain around his neck. As far as Pharaoh is concerned, Joseph's decisions are his decisions. Joseph had the power and authority to make decisions as if he were Pharaoh. When we are **given** authority we are able to act as if we are that person.

As we grow as sons and daughters I believe we grow in authority. Not an authority which comes from our own strength or determination but an authority that is God-given and borne out of the Spirit living in us. It is not an authority that is proud or arrogant, nor is it driven by selfish ambition. It is an authority which follows the example of Jesus and walks the path of humility, seeking to have the mind of Christ. As we follow Jesus' example, the Father will raise us up so we shine as lights in this dark world and our words and actions will begin to have an impact (Philippians 2).

In my office I put staff in charge of a group of clients and give them the freedom to make decisions and give advice to those clients. I do that because I know they have the right qualifications and experience. Qualification and experience are only part of the picture as the most important thing is that I **know and trust them**. I know how they relate to clients and I know they want to do a good job. I also know that if they reach the limit of their capability they will come to me so we can find a solution together.

A father gives his children authority because he knows who they are and he trusts them to make decisions on his behalf. Because of his love for them he trusts them even when they make mistakes. Making a mistake is not a reason for removing authority, but an opportunity for training, correction and ultimately releasing them into greater freedom.

There is an apparent contradiction between two verses in John's gospel. Both are spoken by Jesus in the final few hours before he is taken away to be crucified; they help to explain the transition of our release into sonship and the authority that follows.

Firstly in John 14:14 Jesus says: *You may ask* ***me*** *for anything in my name, and I will do it*. It's like he becomes a go-between and takes our requests to the Father as we are unable to do it ourselves. He stands in the gap for us.

It's only a couple of chapters later when Jesus says something which, on the face of it, seems to contradict this. In John 16:23 Jesus says: *In that day you will no longer ask* **me** *anything. I tell you the truth, my Father will give you whatever you ask in my name*. Here Jesus is saying that we no longer need a go-between, we can go to the Father ourselves. We now have the same direct access to Father as Jesus has. He re-iterates this in verse 26 by saying *'I will not ask the Father on your behalf'* – we can ask him ourselves.

In John chapters 14-17, Jesus carefully explains the transition which is taking place. Through his death we are reconciled to the Father and once again can have relationship with him. Through his resurrection we too are raised up and seated in the Heavenly places in Christ Jesus. No longer do we need to live like orphans because the Father has given us his Holy Spirit and so allows us to know we are fathered by our true Father. The Spirit of Sonship makes it possible for us to draw near to Father and know that we are part of his family.

Jesus sums it up for us in the last two verses of John 17: *Righteous Father, though the world does not know you, I know you, and they know that you have sent me. I have made you known to them, and will continue to make you known in order that* ***the love you have for me may be in them*** *and that I myself may be in them.* This is what Jesus came for, that we would know we are loved in exactly the same way and with the same intensity of love that Jesus experienced. Through Jesus, we share the same relationship with his Father so that we may become one with him.

The apparent contradiction I referred to is not a contradiction at all. It's like being shown a before and after photograph. John 14 tells us what it was like before, when we needed a go-between, whereas John 16 shows us what it is like now. We have unlimited and direct access to the Father because of what Jesus did through his death and resurrection. As sons and daughters we have the same authority that Jesus has and this is given to us because we belong to the family and have a part to play. Just as the younger son had his authority restored, we too are entrusted with authority that flows out of our relationship with Father. We can act on his behalf because his Spirit is living in us.

I believe there is one further key which Jesus provides us with as he explains this transition. Why has this taken place? The answer is in John 16:27 – **"the Father himself loves you"**. This may be one of the most powerful statements in the Bible. Because of his great love for us, he has made it possible for us to join his family and to share in the intimate and glorious relationship of the Trinity. **We** have access to the Father and can ask him anything in Jesus' name.

Let me add a word or two about asking for things in Jesus' name. It does not mean we end our prayers by slightly raising our voice and saying in an authoritarian tone "in Jesus name, AMEN". The words themselves are not a formula for seeing the will of God come about through our prayers; it's certainly not the level or tone of our voice that will make him act!

When Jesus instructs us to pray in his name he means that we pray as if he is praying. What we know as the Lord's prayer shows us what Jesus means. When we pray, we come to our Father and then we ask him to show us his will in order that we might see it come on earth. Jesus only did what he saw his Father doing; the words he spoke were not his words but his Father's words. Our lives are now hidden in Christ so when we pray in his name we are speaking to our Father from the place of 'in-ness'. We are speaking to him in the same way as Jesus would, which is from a heart of wanting to please him and desiring to see his will being done. We are given authority to see the will of Heaven being done on earth through us. Praying in Jesus' name is part of the fulfillment of walking as Jesus walked. This is the authority that is given to us as we walk as sons and daughters.

The writer of Hebrews gives us further insight into the authority which is entrusted to us. The first two chapters of Hebrews draw together a series of Old Testament prophecies about Jesus and the authority he has been given by his Father. The emphasis throughout is on him being a son and not a servant.

We are reminded that in the past God spoke to his people through the prophets but now he speaks to us through someone who is exactly like him, his own son Jesus. Jesus, the perfect son, is crowned with glory and honour. He is seated on a throne which is established for all eternity and has had everything made subject to him as he rules with authority.

As we read these two chapters we see the amazing authority which belongs to Jesus: he is the heir of all things, the creator of the world, he is exactly like his Father as he radiates glory, he is anointed with gladness, he has power over sin and death and is able to set us free from slavery and death. This Son can sustain everything and anything in the universe by the power of his word. He has accomplished everything that needed to be done for our salvation and, with no more to be done, he sits down at the right hand of the Father in Heaven. He is completely consistent and everlasting. He loves righteousness and hates anything that is wicked. In short, he is in charge of everything. That's authority!

Most of these things are said of Jesus in Hebrews 1 and then the second chapter starts with the words *"therefore we must pay closer attention to what we have heard"*. There is something in these verses for us as well. We see a glimpse of it later in the chapter when we read that many sons are being brought to glory. As Paul says in Romans 8:29 Jesus was the firstborn of many brothers. Jesus has gone before us and made the way for us to share his inheritance with him.

All the things I have mentioned about Jesus are also for us. He has set us free from the yoke of slavery and brought us into his family in order that we might become heirs of the Father, made in his image. We radiate the Father's glory and are anointed with gladness. As we grow to be like Jesus we will begin to love righteousness and hate wickedness.

As we become like Jesus we will also grow in authority which, as I've mentioned, is neither self seeking nor arrogant and is certainly not based on our human ability. The authority we have is given to us, rather than being grasped or sought after. It comes out of relationship.

A friend of mine, Ingrid Wilts, runs a retreat centre on the banks of the River Nile in Uganda and has written a book telling her story of 25 years in Africa[1]. There was one occasion when armed robbers came to her compound in the middle of the night and as they demanded money from Ingrid they shot her in the arm. They continued to demand money and raised their guns ready to shoot again. Ingrid, fearing for her life but knowing the power of God within her, shouted at the top of her voice "In the name of Jesus, you people, go, go go". Maybe it was ok on this occasion to use a raised voice! Needless to say the armed gunman fled leaving Ingrid to seek urgent medical help for her wounded arm.

In Ingrid's book there are many stories of her needing to use the authority that Father gives to his sons and daughters. Sometimes she was fearing for her life, other times she needed to see supernatural provision. There are times when we need to shake off our timidity and use our authority to stand in the spirit of love and power and see the will of Heaven being done on earth.

In Matthew 8 a Roman Centurion comes to Jesus and asks him to heal his servant. Jesus says six simple words, *'I will go and heal him'*, through which the Centurion recognises Jesus' authority. It is so clear to the soldier that Jesus is a man with authority that he replies:

> *"Lord, I do not deserve to have you come under my roof. But just say the word, and my servant will be healed. For I myself am a man under authority, with soldiers under me. I tell this one, 'Go,' and he goes; and that one, 'Come,' and he comes. I say to my servant, 'Do this,' and he does it."* (Matthew 8:8-9)

The Centurion sees something in Jesus and knows instantly that Jesus doesn't have to make the journey to his house. Jesus can simply say the words and they will carry through time and space to heal the servant.

Jesus has such authority that he can go without food for forty days and nights in the desert and still tell the devil where to go. At his command Satan only had one option and that was to leave him alone.

Whenever Jesus healed people he had no need to shout loudly as if to wake up the evil spirits. All he needed to do was to speak calmly and say 'be healed' or 'your faith has made you well'. Authority is something inside us. It has been given to us because we are the Father's children and he wants us to act on his behalf. He wants to see Heaven come on earth and whilst he could intervene and do it himself, he chooses to use us, his family.

When Jesus spoke to people, he spoke to their hearts in order to set them free. The authority we have is a gift to bring freedom to ourselves and to others. Our Father does not want us to remain prisoners, but he wants our hearts to be free **AND** he wants to use us in setting other captive hearts free. A servant has no authority, he is *under* authority. A son or daughter has authority because they belong to the Father's family and he has given them the right to act on his behalf. The less we recognise our sonship the more our authority is likely to be self-centred. In fact, it may seek more to control than to release people into freedom. As we grow in sonship our hearts are filled with the Father's love and we change from acting for our own benefit to acting for his glory.

Towards the beginning of this chapter I mentioned the authority which had been given to Joseph. Hopefully we are familiar with the story: he had been sold into slavery by his brothers, languished in prison for something he had not done and then, many years later, he was appointed Prime Minister of Egypt. During the time of famine Joseph's brothers come looking for food as their own supplies have run out. When they appear before Joseph they do not recognise him as their long lost brother.

Joseph has the power to punish his brothers. He has the power to hold them to account and see human justice handed out. But during his time away from home something has happened in his heart. Instead of using his power to punish, he uses it to bring restoration and to provide for those he loves. He uses his authority not for judgment but for blessing.

Sons and daughters belong to the family and are therefore free. They have a quiet confidence in who they are which enables them to listen to their Father and then speak his word with boldness. When that happens freedom comes. We do not have our own authority but are entrusted with the Father's authority which we can steward and use in accordance with his will and purposes. Whenever we exercise authority we do so for the benefit of others in order that they may be set free and released into their identity and destiny. Instead of judgment we can seek blessing.

At the start of his ministry Jesus quoted the prophet Isaiah:

> *"The Spirit of the Lord is on me, because he has anointed me to proclaim good news to the poor. He has sent me to proclaim freedom for the prisoners and recovery of sight for the blind, to set the oppressed free, to proclaim the year of the Lord's favour."* (Luke 4:18-19)

Because he had been anointed he had authority to set the captives free, heal the sick and to declare to those who were oppressed that they now lived in a time of God's favour. When we are filled with the Spirit we are anointed in the same way (2 Corinthians 1:21). We are not only given authority but we are enabled by the Spirit to do the work of the Father and consequently we will see captives being set free, the sick healed and those who suffer being shown favour.

As we live in love we will discover that we have been given the authority belonging to sons and daughters. This is a quiet authority which comes from our knowledge of who we truly are. Like the son in Luke 15, we have experienced a homecoming into the safe and welcome arms of our Father.

NOTE:

1. *River in the Heart* by Ingrid Wilts, published by Verlag Gottfried Bernard: ISBN 978-3-941714-19-9

Chapter 8

Working in the Father's Business

> *"God blessed them and said to them, 'Be fruitful and increase in number; fill the earth and subdue it. Rule over the fish in the sea and the birds in the sky and over every living creature that moves on the ground'."* (Genesis 1:28)

In the story of Creation, even before the fall of Adam and his wife there are three or four references to work. Having created mankind, God told them to be fruitful and multiply, to fill the earth and to rule over it. When the story is told again in Genesis 2 we read that there were no plants because 'there was no man to **work** the ground' (verse 5). Once creation was finished God takes the man and puts him in the Garden of Eden in order to 'work it and keep it' (Genesis 2:15). Work was clearly meant to be important and something we should be actively involved in.

All too often we view work as part of the curse, which we believe was put on us in the garden after Adam and his wife were 'found out'. We think work is something we have to do as part of the punishment for disobeying God. If we view work as a punishment we will always be trying to win God's favour by seeking to put right what had previously gone wrong

Let me deal with a few misconceptions that this interpretation highlights.

Firstly, we were not cursed. When God, our Father, had the discussion with Adam and his wife after they had sinned, he did not put a curse on them. He told them what the consequences of their actions would be but he did not curse them. He cursed Satan and he cursed the ground which man would work. But God, as a loving Father, did not, could not and would not curse his children.

Secondly, work is not something we have to do in order to please God. Work was ordained as part of God's plan, to be something which would be fulfilling, fruitful and a blessing to others. Work is meant to be a good thing which is why Paul condemns idleness and says 'if anyone is not willing to work, let him not eat' (2 Thessalonians 3:10). Our view of work causes us to become worn out and consumed by a performance driven attitude of trying to please God and others. When we understand that through Jesus everything that needs to be done has been done, we will rediscover the right attitude towards work which enables us to be at rest and to rule as God intended. This rest and authority grows in us as we live as sons and daughters who work for a Father, rather than being slaves trying to please a master.

Thirdly, we have adopted a Greek mentality which separates the work we do for a living from the work we do for God. We have therefore created the concept of 'ministry' and made this a separate part of our lives. God sees us as a whole person and does not see this false divide we have invented. The Hebrew mindset sees us holistically and therefore sees the work we do for a living as being as important as anything else we may do or be involved in. There is no sacred/secular divide in God's eyes and I therefore do not want to separate the work we do 'for God' from the work we do for a living. To do so creates a false divide and can devalue the work which is done so ably by many people, but which is often viewed as being done 'in the world'. Somehow we have inflated the work we do 'for the Church' and by implication 'for the Lord' and made that more valuable than the work done by the majority of us.

We are just as capable of doing a good job as a school teacher or nurse as we are when working in Christian ministry. We are just as capable of being driven or striving for acceptance in the workplace or the family as we are in our Christian life. What I want to focus on in this chapter is a heart attitude towards whatever work we have been called to do. The work Adam was given in the garden was very practical; it was stewarding the land and making it fruitful. It was that same work which became a burden after the fall, but I believe we can be free of that burden and see our work restored to God's original and only plan.

To be clear, **everything** we do, we do for Him.

> *"**Whatever you do**, work at it with all your heart, as working for the Lord, not for*

> *human masters, since you know that you will receive an inheritance from the Lord as a reward.* ***It is the Lord Christ you are serving.****" (Colossians 3:23-24)*

Work, for many people, has become a means to an end. It has become something through which we try and discover our identity. We try and use work to fill the hole inside of us that can ultimately only be filled with the love of the Father.

There is one final mention of work in the opening chapters of Genesis:

> *"By the seventh day God had finished the work he had been doing; so on the seventh day he rested from all his work." (Genesis 2:2)*

His work was complete; it was now over to us. The genealogy in Luke's gospel ends with Adam being called the son of God. God rested from his work and handed it over to his son, Adam. It is not so common these days, but there used to be a lot of small businesses which were called, for example, Smith and Sons, or Jones and Son. Sons would learn a trade and then take over the family business which would be passed from one generation to the next. There is a company in the UK which makes beautiful leather bound bibles and is now in the fourth generation of the same family. Sadly the days of a family business are nearly behind us, but this was the model God instigated in the garden. Work was always meant to be done out of relationship.

As we know, Adam was unable to pass onto his sons what God had originally intended. Part of the consequence of Adam's sin was that work became a burden. This burden increased after Cain killed his brother, Abel. When God talked with Cain about what had happened, he said the ground would no longer be so fruitful (Genesis 4:12). The blessing and fruitfulness of work diminished as the burden and effort of work took over.

The story of the two sons in Luke 15 is in part a story of a family business. As we have seen in earlier chapters neither son had the heart of sonship and therefore neither son was able to work out of relationship. One son left to do his own thing and the other son lived as slave. Yes, they were part of the business, but in their hearts they were not part of the family.

There is another son who is able to work in his Father's business out of rest. He is fruitful and a blessing to others. This other son is so focused on pleasing his Father that he only does the things his Father gives him to do. This son, of course, is Jesus. He showed us what a life looks like when a son truly works in the family business. He shows a life that is not based on striving, that is not driven nor seeks to gain self-acceptance through work. He shows us what a life of peace and rest really looks like. He worked hard and was busy, but describes his yoke as being light and easy. He knew what it meant to please his Father whether it was paying the taxes, feeding the 5000, healing the sick or comforting those in distress.

We have become a very busy people. Families, work and church all compete for our limited time and resources. It often feels like a struggle to keep our heads above water and do the minimum needed to survive. We buy a new calendar at the start of a year and our annual holidays become a marker; a finishing line we have to limp over and then we can collapse for a couple of weeks. This is a long way from the life we are encouraged to lead, when the writer of Hebrews encourages us to enter the rest God has prepared for us. It is a long way from the life Jesus offers us in Matthew 11, when he says 'come to me and I will give you rest'. Somehow our busyness has consumed us and pulled us away from the life God intended us to live.

David puts his finger on the problem in Psalm 95 when he says 'our hearts have gone astray' as we have not known his ways. Consequently we are 'unable to enter our rest'. Our hearts have become distracted through pain or wounding, through seeking pleasure or affirmation or through striving and trying to win favour and please God with our activity.

How can we see God's original intention being restored?

Jeremiah gives us a simple clue: we need to stop and consider.

> *"This is what the Lord says: 'Stand at the crossroads and look; ask for the ancient paths, ask where the good way is, and walk in it, and you will find rest for your souls.' But you said, 'We will not walk in it'." (Jeremiah 6:16)*

We are given a choice, but before we can make that choice we need to **stop and consider**. Jeremiah implies there are several paths we could take, but he asks us to look for the 'good' way and then walk in it. The result is we begin to find the rest for our souls which Jesus promises us in Matthew 11. We can recover what we have lost.

In Matthew 11 Jesus' disciples come to him and ask if he is the Messiah. He replies 'what are you seeing, look at the miracles'. The implication is that Jesus' work speaks for itself. His actions show who he really is. He concludes the chapter with the well known passage about his yoke being easy and his burden light. But take note, this passage starts with the words:

> *I praise you, Father, Lord of heaven and earth, because you have hidden these things from the wise and learned, and revealed them to little children. Yes, Father, for this is what you were pleased to do. (Matthew 11:25-26)*

What we are desperately seeking is hidden and will only be revealed to those with a childlike heart. In fact, it is his pleasure to reveal these secrets to those with a childlike heart, whereas they remain hidden from the so called wise and learned. We spend a lot of our time becoming wise and learned, but Father is looking for a simplicity of heart and a dependence on him that allows us to see who he really is. Jesus often used a child to demonstrate what our hearts needed to be like if we are to enter his Kingdom. In Matthew 18 he took a child and said that to enter the Kingdom we need to change (turn completely around), humble ourselves and become like a child.

Jesus focuses us back on the truth. The only way for us to find the place of rest we are seeking is for the Father to be revealed to us. As the Father is revealed we find a contentment and a rest for our souls. It is all about our hearts. Work becomes a burden when we stop doing it out of relationship with Him, but rather do it from our own strength and ability. We have relied on being 'wise and learned' rather than depending on him. Self dependence and self provision are hallmarks of an orphan way of life where we believe we are the answer to our problems. If you read Lamentations 5 you will see an orphan way of life where God's blessing has been replaced by striving and where relationship has been replaced by isolation. This is the heavy yoke Jesus promises to lift off us.

I mentioned at the start of the chapter that I don't want to separate the work we do for a living from the work we do for God. We can't make 'the Lord's work' more valuable than our paid job. In the previous chapter I wrote about the authority which is given to sons and daughters. This authority, given to us by the Father, is to be exercised in every area of our life. There is no divide between secular and spiritual; in everything we do we are always his sons and daughters.

In my job I meet Christians from all walks of life who are weighed down, worn out and wondering where God's blessing is. Whether they are accountants, church workers, running a factory or being a consultant, they can be as worn out trying to please God with their activity as much on the shop floor Monday through to Friday as in the church in the evening and at weekends.

Whatever we do needs to be done out of rest. It can only be done out of rest if it is done out of relationship. The story of Cain shows us the despair of a working life which has become a burden. Cain's life has become hard as there is opposition to fruitfulness. He has been told he will be a 'restless wanderer on the face of the earth'. Instead of our work being a blessing we have allowed it to become a striving, competitive way of life where we seek dominance and control. This is a long way from the Father's intention.

A life of rest is not a life of laziness or inactivity. A life of rest is a heart attitude, where we learn to walk as Jesus walked by listening to what Father is calling us to do. Everything we do needs to be motivated by the love of God. If you are a teacher or a nurse, if you work at home with your children, if you run a business – all of these things are as important as being a pastor in the church. Do them all from a heart of love. You may have a bad boss but that is not the issue here. We need to seek to do a good job and honour our employer, but ultimately everything we do must come from a heart which wants to please our Heavenly Father. We are seeking to please him and through our lives bring a bit of Heaven to earth.

We often talk about striving and being performance driven; somehow we think those characteristics are limited to our Christian life or ministry. We can't divorce one part of our life from another. If we are striving in our Christian work we are probably striving at our workplace. As we live in love his peace will fill our hearts and as it does every part of our life will be affected. As our heart is filled with peace and rest everything we do will change. When we walk round the office, the factory or our college we will be different. His presence living in us will flow out of us to those around us. It will affect and change our work places, our homes and our churches.

I have seen this first hand. The three of us who run our business are Christians and we seek to pray together most Monday mornings. We ask that God will fill us and the office with his peace. We have had all sorts of people remark on how peaceful our office is – from the postmen, to staff and clients.

Living in love will change us. It will change the places we live and work. As we live in love we begin to see the Kingdom of Heaven come to earth. The blessing and fruitfulness of our work has been stolen from us and so we have fallen into the ways of the world. We have settled for striving, competition and productivity based on achievement, rather than seeing our work being done out of relationship with Father which will lead to fruitfulness and blessing. As we grow in living in love, we can regain the blessing of work because whatever we do we will be doing for our Father. There is no sacred/secular divide. Everything we do is an expression of who we are and growing in sonship will lead to us expressing the Father's heart to the world around us.

Let me finish with some words of Jesus:

> *"And slaves have no permanent standing in a family, like a son does, for a son is part of the family forever. So if the revelation of being a son sets you free from sin, then become a true son and be unquestionably free." (John 8:35-36 The Passion Translation)*

> *"You are my friends if you do what I command. I no longer call you servants, because a servant does not know his master's business. Instead, I have called you friends, for everything that I learned from my Father I have made known to you. You did not choose me, but I chose you and appointed you so that you might go and bear fruit – fruit that will last – and so that*

whatever you ask in my name the Father will give you." (John 15:14-16)

We have his Spirit in us who causes us to walk in his ways. What that looks like will be different for each one of us. Whatever it is for you, do it with your whole heart, do it from the place of rest where you know who your Father is. Do it from a heart of love, not because you have to, but because you want to please him.

The Father's business has many expressions – what does yours look like?

> **"IN THE SAME WAY, LET YOUR LIGHT SHINE BEFORE OTHERS, SO THAT THEY MAY SEE YOUR GOOD WORKS AND GIVE GLORY TO YOUR FATHER WHO IS IN HEAVEN."** (Matthew 5:16 ESV)

Chapter 9

Walking as Jesus Walked

> *"Whoever says "I know him" but does not keep his commandments is a liar, and the truth is not in him, but whoever keeps his word, in him truly the love of God is perfected. By this we may know that we are in him: whoever says he abides in him ought to walk in the same way in which he walked."* (1 John 2:4-6 ESV)

John is pretty direct here. If we claim to belong to God but don't do as he commands we are a liar or a hypocrite! That's a very blunt statement. John doesn't pull his punches as he goes on to say that if we claim to be a part of him then we ***ought*** to live like Jesus. It's easy for us to miss the point, and the heart, of what John is saying if we purely read the words without understanding the context in which they have been written. It would be easy to interpret John's words as a new set of commands or rules by which we should live.

As I mentioned in chapter 5, there are some things I should do in order to keep myself on the right side of the law. Failure to do so will land me with a penalty or a punishment. There are other things I should **want** to do in order to avoid broken relationships, particularly with those I love. It is in this latter context that John writes his letter. He is not setting out a new law or a set of regulations by which we should live, but he is showing us the things we will **want** to do if our heart is to please our Heavenly Father.

As we read through John's letter we see it is full of relationship. The very first verse of the letter describes how he has seen, heard and touched the things that he is writing about. He has known the extravagant love of the Father and is desperate for us to experience this love-filled relationship where we know the Father is loving us now. He encourages us to come into fellowship (relationship) with the Father and his son, Jesus (1 John 1:3) and to live a life in harmony with him. At the start of chapter 3 John reminds us of the love which has been lavished on us and he emphasises that we are God's children – "*....and that is what we are*" (1 John 3:1).

Everything John writes is in the context of relationship.

When he encourages us to walk as Jesus walked he is showing us what this relationship looks like. It is not something we do because we have to, but it is because we choose to live in relationship with the Father. No intimate relationship can be governed by a set of rules.

As you read further through this chapter I urge you to remember that everything needs to be put in this relational context.

Walking as Jesus walked is not drawing up a list of all the things he did and then trying to copy them. That would be legalistic and you would create for yourself a lifestyle which would be practically unattainable. Walking as Jesus walked is having fellowship and oneness with the Father in the same way as Jesus did.

Before I mention a few of the things which John shows us I want to look at the fruit of the Spirit in Galatians 5:

> *"But the fruit of the Spirit is love, joy, peace, forbearance, kindness, goodness, faithfulness, gentleness and self-control. Against such things there is no law."* (verses 22-23)

This well known passage shows us what it is like when we walk as Jesus walked. He lived his life in perfect and complete love, perfect and complete joy, peace, patience, kindness and so on. As we are transformed into his likeness, love will begin to express itself in our lives through more of the fruit of the Spirit being manifest.

Let me quote these verses again, this time from the Passion Translation:

> *But the fruit of the Holy Spirit within you is divine love in all its various expressions. This love is revealed through:*
>
> *Joy that overflows*
> *Peace that subdues*
> *Patience that endures*
> *Kindness on display*

> *A life full of virtue*
> *Faith that prevails*
> *Gentleness of heart and*
> *Strength of spirit*
>
> *Never set the law above these qualities, for they are meant to be limitless.* Galatians 5:22-23 (The Passion Translation)

Whilst we may not attain the same perfect expression of love as Jesus, it is true that living in love will cause the fruit of the Spirit to multiply within us. This is part of the abundant and lasting fruit which John writes about in chapter 15 of his gospel. Fruit, by nature, starts off as a small seed which grows until it is ready for harvest. The fruit of the Spirit is only part of the fruit we are to bear as everything we do or are involved in should grow and increase. This is the original mandate given to Adam and his wife in the garden: 'be fruitful and multiply'.

Fruit does not come from following a set of rules but it is the expression of *'divine love'* resulting from relationship with the Father. It is the consequence of our fellowship and oneness with him.

When we walk as Jesus walked, we are changed from one degree of glory to another so that we become like him.

I want to highlight a few things from John's letter which show us what walking like Jesus looks like. Before you read on, remind yourself that everything John wrote was in the context of relationship.

It is not possible for light and darkness to cohabit! Not only is God love, but he is also light. We are encouraged to live in the light with Father, and with one another, by bringing things out into the open. We don't need to talk about the deep things of our heart with everyone but we do need a few close friends with whom we can share at a deep level. When we share the 'stuff' of our lives, we do it for the purpose of clearing out the rubbish in order that we can enjoy a greater depth of relationship and more freedom. God, our Father, never condemns us but is always ready to forgive and to cleanse us.

If we have an overwhelming desire for relationship we will **want** to walk away from sin. Instead of focussing on the rubbish in our lives we will see what we really need and that is relationship with Father. This will cause us to walk towards him. John recognises that no one is free from sin, but he encourages us to be sensitive to sin in order that we are quick to confess and allow the Father to cleanse our conscience. When we sin against someone it causes broken relationships and by walking in the light with one another we can see those relationships restored quickly.

Walking in the light is about right relationships; firstly with Father and then with each other. As we walk in the light we are able to walk freely and lightly as the burden is lifted from us. It has nothing to do with condemnation but is a way for us to enter the glorious freedom of the children of God.

Having shown us that walking in the light is to walk as Jesus walked, John then gives us a choice of lovers:

> *"Do not love the world or anything in the world. If anyone loves the world, love for the Father is not in them. For everything in the world – the lust of the flesh, the lust of the eyes, and the pride of life – comes not from the Father but from the world. The world and its desires pass away, but whoever does the will of God lives for ever."* (1 John 2:15-17)

Again, John's choice of words appears very strong. He presents a stark contrast between loving the Father and loving the world. One is temporary and the other lasts for eternity. There is nothing wrong with having nice things or living in a nice house but if they become the focus of our attention then we have taken our gaze off the Father. There are other things which are more harmful than possessions and John refers to these as the 'lust of the flesh and the lust of the eyes'. The eyes are the gateway of our soul and we can easily taint or pollute our heart by looking at or spending time on the wrong things.

Jesus said it is not possible for us to serve two masters. If we love the pleasures of the world or the evil of the world we will not be able to fully love him.

John's words are strong. He is giving us a choice and in doing so he urges us to choose the Father's will, which is ultimately for our eternal good. When we remember that he says this in the context of relationship and us growing in fellowship and oneness with the Father it is easier to make the choice between these two lovers. Why would we choose to love the world when receiving and growing in the eternal love of the Father is the other option?

I don't want to over simplify this as I am fully aware of the struggles we all face. Whilst the contrast between these two lovers is clear it will inevitably be a process of change and transition which results in the transformation of our hearts. Over time you will notice there has been a shift in your heart away from the ways of the world to the ways of God's heart. Though the journey may take time, I encourage you not to give up but to keep turning your eyes towards Father and pursuing him. He's worth it!

Our sonship has to have an expression and a practical outworking in our lives. I believe these two areas are important as we grow into maturity as sons and daughters, because as we walk like Jesus there will be a deepening of our heart connection to the Father.

In chapter 7 I wrote about the authority of sons and daughters and so I don't need to go over that again. Suffice to say, in 1 John 2:27, we are reminded that the Father has given his authority to us which enables us to call the things of Heaven down to earth. Generally a king does not entrust his authority to slaves, but he gives it to his sons and daughters who have a heart to please him. In Matthew 6 Jesus prayed that the Father's will would be done on earth just as it is done in Heaven. As we begin to walk as Jesus walked we grow in anointing and authority; not because we have grasped it for ourselves, but because the Father trusts us to act on his behalf. The Kingdom of Heaven is not an elusive thing that we struggle to understand but it is a king reigning in love who allows us, as the Father's sons and daughters, to share in his government. We are invited to partake in the Father's business and are entrusted with the keys and secrets of his kingdom.

When Samuel anointed David as the future king we read that the Holy Spirit rushed on him and he was filled with power. It is the same for us. As we live as anointed sons and daughters the Holy Spirit will fill us with power and equip us to see the Father's will accomplished.

As I have mentioned it is a journey for us to learn to walk as Jesus walked. It is not necessarily something that happens overnight. It's like there is a seed that has been planted which will take root and grow. Just as the fruit of the Spirit grows in us, so the spirit of sonship will also grow. John reminds us that we are God's children **NOW** (1 John 3:1) but goes on to point out that there is still much more to come. He tells us what we **will be** has not yet been revealed. We are sons and daughters, that is our true identity, but there is a greater revelation of who we really are for us to grow into. There is a greater revelation and depth of the Father's love for us to receive. As we grow in love we begin to realise that the Father's love really is limitless and that it will never run out. If the Father's love is an ocean we have only experienced a bucketful so far.

Jesus was connected to the source of love all the time. As we live in him we are also connected to the source of love as God, our Father, is love. His love will never fail us, it will never let us down and there is always more. In Ephesians 3:18 Paul prays that we would understand the vastness and totality of the Father's love and therefore begin to see how it can transform us to be like Jesus. All John can say as he tries to explain this, is that it will change us to be like him (1 John 3:2) and we shall begin to reflect his glory.

I thought it was enough when I understood that I was a son and that God was my Father. As time has gone on I realise how vast a revelation it is and how much more there is for me to grow into. I can agree with John; I know I am his child but I am looking forward to seeing a whole lot more being revealed to me and in me.

As this seed grows, love will begin to be the hallmark of our lives. The love that John writes about is something for us to experience. Love is not a collection of facts that we store in our mind but it is an experience that comes out of relationship. John tells us that we can know and rely on the love that God has for us (1 John 4:16). These are experiential words that have substance because we have proved them to be true and seen the fruit of them in our lives. This is not about acquiring head knowledge, it is building a wealth of experience where we have known and been able to trust the love of God. Our experience and our walk with Father enable us to have a 'love bank' which contains a rich deposit of history with him.

The love of the Father goes beyond our understanding. If we ever get our minds around it then we have minimised it and made it too small. On one level we will never fully understand his love, but equally the more we experience it the more it becomes a part of us. This is the childlike heart that Jesus encourages us to have where we are totally dependent on him and simply believe that he is enough.

As the seed of love grows in our heart, fear has to leave. Fear and love are incompatible and can't exist alongside each other. Thankfully love is stronger and can drive the fear out of our hearts. Jesus lived his whole life in love and we too can make it our dwelling place where love becomes the hallmark of who we are and what we do.

The Message describes it like this:

> *"God is love. When we take up permanent residence in a life of love, we live in God and God lives in us. This way, love has the run of the house, becomes at home and mature in us, so that we're free of worry on Judgment Day—our standing in the world is identical with Christ's. There is no room in*

> *love for fear. Well-formed love banishes fear. Since fear is crippling, a fearful life—fear of death, fear of judgment—is one not yet fully formed in love."* (1 John 4:17-18 The Message)

John's encouragement throughout his letter is for us to see and embrace the lifestyle of Jesus. He gives us these signposts to help us walk in the same way as Jesus walked. Jesus' life was total fellowship and oneness with the Father and John shows us that it is possible for us to live in the same way. He is not imposing a set of rules but he is showing us what the fruit of relationship with the Father looks like.

* * * * * * * * *

If anyone understood what it meant to walk as Jesus walked it was the Apostle Paul. He had an amazing encounter with the love of God which totally transformed him from being an angry murderer to someone who found his true identity as a son of God. Out of his own experience, he describes for us what it means to live in Christ and therefore to be drawn into relationship with the Trinity. He shows us what it is like to walk as Jesus walked and he gives us a framework to help us achieve this in our own lives. Like John, this framework is not a new set of rules or regulations but is based in and grows out of relationship.

> *"Since, then, you have been raised with Christ, set your hearts on things above,*

> *where Christ is, seated at the right hand of God. Set your minds on things above, not on earthly things. For you died, and your life is now hidden with Christ in God."* (Colossians 3:1-3)

Paul's exhortation is for us to set our hearts **and** minds on the things of Heaven. It is all too easy for us to focus on the stuff of life and the things that confront us every day. In doing so we lose our Heavenly perspective. Paul reminds us that our lives are hidden away with Christ in God and so our destiny and identity are tied up with him rather than the things of this world. We have been brought to life through Christ and Paul calls us to live as the people we really are. A tremendous destiny has been birthed in us and Paul points us in a direction which will allow that destiny to grow and mature in us.

In his opening prayer, Paul starts off by thanking the Father for the faith and love which come from the 'hope stored up for you in heaven'. What a wonderful phrase! All of Heaven is cheering us on, so we can become inspired to see the gospel bearing fruit and growing in us on a daily basis. Paul cannot see us in any other way than being in Christ. This has to mean all the resources of Heaven are made available to us, not only to transform us, but to transform the world in which we live. That's what Jesus experienced in his life – all the resources of Heaven being channelled through him.

It is an exciting life we step into when we allow the life of Heaven to flood us and flow out of us. It is, quite simply, a lot better than the life of this world! We are invited to share in Jesus' inheritance and as we do we begin *'to walk in a manner worthy of the Lord, fully pleasing to him, bearing fruit in every good work and increasing in the knowledge of God'* (Colossians 1:10 ESV). It is important that we set that verse in the context of relationship, otherwise we fall back into striving and performance all of which is motivated by fear rather than by love. When we are motivated by love our heart is to please Father and so become like Jesus.

Walking as Jesus walked will cause us to bear fruit. It will also cause our patience and endurance to grow (Colossians 1:11). I guess we would like to shy away from letting patience and endurance increase; it sounds a bit too much like hard work. But if Jesus could endure the cross because of the joy which was waiting for him on the other side then I hope we can endure the 'momentary and light afflictions' we face regularly. You may have heard the expression: 'when the going gets tough, the tough get going', well there is something positive in that for us. There are times when things are hard, there are seasons when we would like to give up, there are people we would rather not deal with. It's times like this when we have to ask Father for more patience and for endurance to carry us through. As we do, we are led not only to a greater depth of relationship with Father but also to our lives becoming more firmly rooted and established in love.

Let me remind you of these verses in Romans:

> *"Not only so, but we also glory in our sufferings, because we know that suffering produces perseverance; perseverance, character; and character, hope. And hope does not put us to shame, because God's love has been poured out into our hearts through the Holy Spirit, who has been given to us".* (Romans 5:3-5)

Endurance leads to us having hope; a hope that is satisfied because we have come to know that we can rely on and experience his love for us. He will never let us down.

Paul's aim in writing Colossians is that we would *'be encouraged in heart and united in love'* (Colossian 2:2) in order that we would have complete understanding of the mysteries of God. Jesus tells us in Matthew 11 that no one knows the Father except the Son and here Paul reveals that we can grasp *and* understand the mystery of God. That's a lot of mystery for us to comprehend and the very thought of it may feel like a burden to you. As with everything, this has to be read in the context of relationship. After all it is Jesus who reveals the Father to us and enables us to make sense of the journey we are called to be part of. If we try to manage the journey on our own, outside of relationship, we will become worn out or we will fall back into a performance mindset where we strive to achieve and win favour. I do not find either of these alternatives attractive.

If we are to live a life worthy of the Lord then we need to be constantly rooted and built up in him (Colossians 2:7). Consequently our faith grows and we become stronger and more able to resist the ways of the world.

The world has a negative view of maturity. In the eyes of the world, we are mature when we are independent and have reached a certain level of competency. Anyone who is dependent is deemed to be immature and is constantly provoked to 'get their act together'. That is not how Father sees it. True maturity is dependence on him where we live like Jesus, who said:

> *"I tell you, the Son can do nothing by himself; he can do only what he sees his Father doing, because whatever the Father does the Son also does."* (John 5:19)

We spend a lot of our time becoming wise and learned and that is the very thing which prevents us from having the childlike heart needed to enter the Kingdom of Heaven. Father does not want us to remain as infants but he wants us to grow as sons and daughters who will live like his son Jesus. Growing up does not mean we lose our childlike heart, if anything that is something we need to regain. It means that we become more dependent on him and his Spirit so we are not swayed by the 'hollow and deceptive philosophies' of the world. It means we become planted in love so the source of our life is his life within us.

Maturity is having a childlike heart. Maturity is dependence rather than independence. This is how Jesus walked, this is the true heart of sonship.

My friend, Barry Adams, puts it like this: 'The spirit of sonship is Christ in us, so when we walk as Jesus walked we yield to Jesus in us'.

Chapter 10

The Beauty of Process

A while ago whilst driving my car I had a discussion with Father which went something like this:

Me: Why don't you flick the switch and sort everything out instantly?
Father: What would our relationship be like if I did?
Me: Um, I guess it would become automated and clinical.
Father: If I did that you would stop seeking me with your heart.

And then he said this, which at the time was quite a surprise.....

Father: It is the beauty of process that keeps you seeking me and desiring relationship with me.

"The beauty of process". That was not what I was expecting to hear.

It did, of course, leave me with a question: "do I see the process as something beautiful?" Or do I want to get through it as quickly as possible and then move onto the next thing. As we seek to walk as Jesus walked our lives become a process of change where we are being transformed to be like him. Many of you reading this may feel you are stuck in a process that you would rather not be in. The process may be painful, it may take time and you may wonder where God is some (if not all) of the time.

Some of you may be enjoying a season of peace where you feel God's blessing on your life. That too is part of the process.

My question to us all is "can we see this as being something beautiful?"

Our encounter with Father is not a one-off event. It is a lifelong journey where we freely choose, even through our ups and downs, to become more and more like Jesus. As I said in the previous chapter it is not a case of drawing up a list of all the things Jesus **did** and then using that as a checklist for our own lives. It is seeking to have the same heart and attitude as he had. We forgive, but then we need to go on forgiving. We walk in forgiveness. We open our heart and then we keep opening our heart. We receive love and go on receiving love. We receive comfort and then need to go on being comforted.

As our journey continues, we can know and experience God being a Father **TO** us every day. When we see the process as a relationship with our Father it is easier for us to see it as something beautiful.

Yet on our journey it sometimes feels as if Father is hiding from us. If he is so loving why does he hide? Well, I believe it is because he wants us to seek him. He does not force himself on us but always leaves us to take the initiative. If he forced the relationship, it would be coercion rather than an expression of pure love.

In Psalm 27 David gives us a glimpse of this 'hide and seek'.

> *"One thing I ask from the Lord, this only do I seek: that I may dwell in the house of the Lord all the days of my life, to gaze on the beauty of the Lord and to seek him in his temple. For in the day of trouble he will keep me safe in his dwelling; he will hide me in the shelter of his sacred tent and set me high upon a rock. Then my head will be exalted above the enemies who surround me; at his sacred tent I will sacrifice with shouts of joy; I will sing and make music to the Lord."* (Psalm 27:4-6)

Our Father wants us to have a longing in our heart to be with him and therefore to seek him with all our heart. As we find him he shows us his beauty and reveals his heart to us. As we find him we are drawn into a safe place where he can hide us in the midst of our troubles. He takes us and hides us from our enemies in a place where we are safe and secure, where we are tucked away under the covering of his protection. Not only does he hide us in a safe place, but he also lifts us up and places us on a rock, high above our enemies and well out of their reach. Effectively he is showing us off. We are safe, yet on show.

He wants us to seek him in order that we can be found by him and then, in the safety of his presence, he lifts us above our troubles, worries and concerns. We are not alone on this journey as he is with us in the midst of this process. When we see this process as being a relationship then it starts to become beautiful. The process is not a problem we have to solve by finding the right solution or doing the right thing. It is a relationship and a journey together. It is the key to our deliverance.

> *"You are my hiding-place; you will protect me from trouble and surround me with songs of deliverance."* (Psalm 32:7)

Let's take a look at Psalm 42 and discover some things about the process and see how it can become a thing of beauty.

The Psalm starts with the longing of David's heart *"As the deer pants for streams of water, so my soul pants for you, my God. My soul thirsts for God, for the living God"*. This is a story of passion and desire where David knows that his life comes directly from his relationship with God, his Father.

Despite his desire, he is in crisis.

> *"My tears have been my food day and night, while people say to me all day long, 'Where is your God?'"* (verse 3)

> *"Why, my soul, are you downcast? Why so disturbed within me? Put your hope in God, for I will yet praise him, my Saviour and my God. My soul is downcast within me; therefore I will remember you from the land of the Jordan, the heights of Hermon – from Mount Mizar."* (verses 5-6)

We can identify with how he is feeling. There are times when it seems as if our tears have become our friend and we wonder where God is. It feels as if we are left to struggle on our own and that God has abandoned us. In the midst of this, our enemies taunt us saying: "Where is your God?" (verse 10). Before we move on, we must recognise that our enemies are not necessarily those people around us. They may be being used as an instrument but we have a real enemy who uses situations and who lies to our mind, will and emotions. Satan comes to steal, kill and destroy as he is the father of lies. He seeks to sow a destructive message into the core of our being and so divert us from our journey with Father.

David recognised he was in a crisis and like him we have to acknowledge the place we are in. Our prayer, or the cry of our heart, can be: "Yes, this season is bad, really bad. But even in this situation I want to, and need to, receive from you. Father I am desperate for you". When we recognise we are in need we can let go of our striving and surrender to him. Jesus reminded us that when we are at the end of ourselves he can step in:

> *'You're blessed when you're at the end of your rope. With less of you there is more of God and his rule."* (Matthew 5:3 The Message)

If we want the process to be a thing of beauty, the first thing we need to do is to accept the reality of our situation and start seeking him. He can then take us into his safe place and lift us above our situation. He will keep us safe.

The second thing David does in Psalm 42 is to remember.

> *"These things I remember as I pour out my soul: how I used to go to the house of God under the protection of the Mighty One with shouts of joy and praise among the festive throng."* (verse 4)

He remembers the 'good old days' when he used to lead the people in worship and praise. He remembers feeling and experiencing the presence of God. He remembers that God is faithful and that his love endures forever. He has known the love of God and he knows, therefore, that he can rely on it once again. God is good, always good. When you read the book of Lamentations you realise the writer is having a bad day. In fact, it may be a bad month, year or even years. Not much is going right for him. But he too remembers the loving kindness and goodness of God. He knows that the faithful love of God never fails and that his mercies are new every morning (Lamentations 3:21-22).

Our past experience of God should not be written off. It is the thing that gives us hope for both the present and the future. We do not need to live in the past, but remembering God's faithful love is important and necessary when we are stuck in the process. Knowing his faithfulness helps us see the process as beautiful as we can trust him to take us forward. David believed that, one day, he would again lead the people in praise and worship. He decides that he will praise again (verse 5) and the passion and longing in his heart will drive him forward. Once again, we see that the basis of this journey is relationship based on love.

Having acknowledged the place he is in, and remembered the faithful love of Father, David cries out.

> *"Deep calls to deep in the roar of your waterfalls; all your waves and breakers have swept over me."* (verse 7)

As we take the step of acknowledging our own situation and remembering Father's loving kindness we too are able to cry out. We may feel we are being overwhelmed by our circumstances but we can still have a longing in our heart for Father and his presence. He longs to be found by us; in fact he is never really hidden. It is like a father playing hide and seek with a young child. When the father goes and hides he does not cover himself but remains 'see-able' so his child can easily find him.

Instead of hiding behind a large oak tree he 'hides' behind a slender silver birch where he is more exposed than hidden. Our Father is not hidden away but the moment our desire is awakened it is he who turns and finds us. As we cry out to him he comes and takes us into that safe place where we are secure and he can lift us above the situations we face. Instead of being taunted by our enemies, he shows us off in front of them.

It takes humility to cry out. We have to accept that we are not the answer to our problem but we need someone outside of us to ride to our rescue.

Finally, David believes.

He believes he will praise God again (verse 5). He puts his trust in the faithful love of the Father (verse 8), once again he chooses to put his hope in Father (verses 5 and 11) and once more he can hear the Father singing over him (verse 8, see also Zephaniah 3:17).

It is the same for us. We can also place our trust in Father and look to him to help us through the process we are in. Father's love is **always** reliable and as we experience it that reliability becomes a foundation in our life. When we have experienced his love we are able to rely on it. Time and time again we can come back to his never ending faithful love and trust him. We can believe that he will lead us into that safe and secure place where we will be lifted above the circumstances we face.

David had hope, and because he had hope he believed. Because he believed he could seek, and because he could seek he could be found. Our definition of hope leaves us with some uncertainty but Biblical hope is a guarantee. We have a guarantee that Father is there with us and will help us through the process.

When we start to see our process being worked out through relationship we can begin to see that it is beautiful.

For all of us there is a process going on whether we recognise it or not. 2 Corinthians 3:18 tells us that we are being changed from one degree of glory to another. That is process or transition, they're really the same thing.

We often talk about transition as if it is something bad or something to be endured. We say the word 'transition' with a groan and with a longing for it to come to an end in order that we can enjoy our lives once again. Yet, when Paul writes about us being transformed from glory to glory he is describing transition, or process. He describes us changing and becoming more glorious than we already are. Whatever stage you are currently at the Father sees you carrying his glory, he is simply looking for that glory to increase. When we see process in this light it is easier for us to see it as something beautiful. We are not being transformed from filthy rags to dirty rags but from **glory** to **glory**.

Transition is not necessarily negative nor a burden instead it can be the very thing which releases us into our destiny. And this destiny is a greater depth of relationship with Father.

Transition, or process, is all around us. I travel to Uganda where the sun sets very quickly. Within about half an hour the sun has gone and the night darkness has come. That is a process, but it is also a time of preparation as the people in the villages get ready for the night. There is limited electricity and no street lights so everything has to be tidied and sorted before darkness falls. A season of process is also a time of preparation as we get ready for what is to come. The process we are in is preparation for a new season where the experiences we have gained can be turned to good. It is preparation for the next level of glory that Father is taking us to and it is part of the process of our lives being transformed into the likeness of Jesus.

Can we see the process as something beautiful?

In Psalm 42 David's focus was on Father. Despite what he was going through he trusted that it was a season in his life that he would be led out of. Sometimes our process is painful, it may be hard and last a long time but we too can have the same heart and attitude as David who was able to write:

> *"As the deer pants for streams of water, so my soul pants for you, my God. My soul thirsts for God, for the living God".*

As we live in love, and learn to walk as Jesus walked, we can start to see the process as being something beautiful because we are walking with Father. We are being hidden in his secret place where we are safe and secure and where he will show us off in front of our enemies. Like David we too can cry out, we can believe and have hope.

The beauty of process is our journey of sonship where we take more confident steps walking as Jesus walked.

Chapter 11

Planted in Love

> *"Then, by constantly using your faith, the life of Christ will be released deep inside you, and the resting place of his love will become the very source and root of your life, providing you with a secure foundation that grows and grows. Then, as your spiritual strength increases, you will empowered to discover the great magnitude of the astonishing love of Christ in all its dimensions."* (Ephesians 3:17-18 The Passion Translation)

It really is possible for us to live in love.

I trust as you have read through this book, you have begun to understand that this is the true destiny for every believer. It is not unattainable nor is it outside of our grasp. We can live in the experience and knowledge that God, the creator of the universe, just happens to be our Father and that he is loving us with the complete and perfect expression of love ***right now***.

In the first few chapters of this book I looked at the way our hearts need to be transformed and changed by the power of his love in order that we become more like Jesus. Walking as Jesus walked is a journey. A journey on which we allow the Father to change us from the inside out and where the pain and wounding of our heart can be healed. It is a journey of transformation, not through our own effort, but by the power of his love working in us.

The second half of the book has been about the way our sonship expresses itself in our everyday lives. These two aspects are not mutually exclusive. We don't have to be perfect with a completely healed heart before our sonship takes on a practical expression. The transformation of our heart and the expression of sonship within us take place at the same time. As our heart changes, we grow in sonship and as we grow in sonship so our heart changes. That's why I talked about process in the previous chapter.

It is as we are planted in love that these two things work in tandem.

In Paul's famous prayer in Ephesians 3 he prays that we would be rooted and established in love, or as the Passion Translation puts it *'the resting place of his love becomes the very source and root of our life'*. Being planted in love is the thing that gives us a solid foundation to life; without it we are swayed from one side to another and tossed about like a boat without an anchor. Before anything, Paul says, we need to be planted in love.

Once we are planted in his love we will begin to understand the magnitude and power of that love. Paul says that the love of the Father is impossible to understand until we are planted or immersed in it. We can't understand it by looking in from the outside. It is not something we measure or assess from the viewpoint of being an observer. To understand it we need to be experiencing and living in it.

It is only as we live in love that we begin to see how vast and totally overwhelming it is. To comprehend the love of God we need to be strengthened. Our human spirit is simply not strong enough to be able to contain the power of this love, it is too much for us. As we are planted in love we receive the strength and ability to understand how immeasurable this love is.

To understand love, we need to be planted in love.

If we are to walk as Jesus walked, we need to be planted in the love of the Father just as Jesus was. I have mentioned several times Jesus' words before he was led away to the cross. We are loved as Jesus is loved:

> *"I have given them the revelation of who you are and I will continue to make you even more real to them, so that they may experience the same endless love that you have for me; for your love will now live in them even as I live in them."* (John 17:26 The Passion Translation)

We read in John 1 that Jesus came from the bosom of the Father. He has always had an intimate relationship and oneness with his Father as he is totally immersed in his Father's love. He lived his whole life in love, only doing his Father's will and only having one motivation which was to please his Father. The roots of his life are deeply planted in love.

This is the legacy that Jesus leaves for us. We can enjoy and live in this same unity with the Father; we too can be deeply planted in love.

How then are we planted in love?

Let me be absolutely clear: the Father is loving you **now**. He has always loved you and there is nothing you or I can do to earn that love. Nothing we ever do causes the Father's love to be turned on (or off, for that matter). It is completely unconditional and totally dependent on him. He does not start loving us when we become Christians as he has had each one of us in his heart and mind since before the creation of the world (Ephesians 1:4). He knew us, and everything about us, before he formed us in our mother's womb (Psalm 139 and Jeremiah 1). As with Adam, **all** of us were conceived in his heart and were born to live in and experience love.

It is not God who needs to change but us!

The fall of mankind and the independence which followed meant that there is now a choice for us each one of us to make. We can respond to the words of John 3:16 *"For this is how much God loved the world – he gave his uniquely conceived Son as a gift. So now everyone who believes in him will never perish, but experience everlasting life"* (The Passion Translation). As we respond to this invitation we are born again and given the right to become children of God (John 1:12). In responding to this invitation, our eternal inheritance and destiny of being with him forever is settled and guaranteed.

But despite being given the right to become sons and daughters, many Christians do not take up that right. Instead of living like Jesus (as sons or daughters) they continue to live as a slave or an orphan. In Luke 15, the Father wanted to treat both sons as true sons but neither could receive it and so they were unable to live in their true identity and inheritance. As we have seen, one son went off and the other remained, living a slavish life of duty and obedience. One son had a change of heart and was able to receive the Father's embrace of love and be restored to the family. So far as the father was concerned both of the boys had always been his sons, it was them who had closed their hearts.

If we are to be planted in love we need the heart of sonship. Without the heart of a son or daughter we remain independent and caught up in our own world of striving and performance, seeking to please a master rather than living in the centre of our Father's affection. In Matthew 18:3 Jesus tells us we need to turn and become like a child, it is as we humble ourselves that we are able to enter his kingdom. The word used for 'turn' means to turn right round and walk in the opposite direction.

I have the privilege of seeing many people receive a revelation of the Father's love. It is always wonderful to see this revelation bring life to people. But I believe there is so much more. A revelation opens our eyes to things we have previously been unable to see. All too often we have a revelation which affects us for a short of period of time but does not change us permanently. Jesus promised us living water that once tasted would mean we do not thirst again (John 4:14). I believe we can experience an impartation of love which will change us forever, so we know we are the beloved sons and daughters of the Father living in the centre of his affection.

This is the transformed life Jesus offered to the people he met. An encounter with Jesus changes lives and just as he changed the life of many people in the gospels so he longs to change our lives too. As we come to Jesus and experience the relationship with Father which he has unveiled, then we too will be changed.

As you read this, you may be feeling that all you have had is a revelation of his love through which you saw something new. You may be longing for something deeper that changes you forever. You don't have to wait until your heart is totally healed (if that were the case none of us would qualify); remember growing in sonship takes place at the same time as our heart is transformed. If this is the longing of your heart – ask him. Ask Father to plant you in his love so that it becomes the very thing which sustains you and causes you to grow as a son or daughter.

You may feel like a little seed but nonetheless you are planted in the extravagant love of the Father. No-one is excluded from this life of love.

In John 17:4 Jesus acknowledges that his job is finished. He has revealed the Father; the true nature of God has once again been shown to mankind. His final prayer is this: *"Father, I ask that you allow everyone you have given to me to reign at our side, for I want them to be where I am!"* (John 17:24 The Passion Translation). This is our true home, with him forever.

As we are planted in love we will begin to understand what the love of the Father is really like. We will start to walk as Jesus walked. We will prove the power of Father's love as we 'know and rely on the love God has for us' (1 John 4:16).

It is an exciting journey we have begun. We are his sons and daughters and it never ceases to amaze me that Father has chosen to make his home in my heart.

> **WHEN I THINK OF ALL THIS, I FALL TO MY KNEES AND PRAY TO THE FATHER, THE CREATOR OF EVERYTHING IN HEAVEN AND ON EARTH. I PRAY THAT FROM HIS GLORIOUS, UNLIMITED RESOURCES HE WILL EMPOWER YOU WITH INNER STRENGTH THROUGH HIS SPIRIT. THEN CHRIST WILL MAKE HIS HOME IN YOUR HEARTS AS YOU TRUST IN HIM. YOUR ROOTS WILL GROW DOWN INTO GOD'S LOVE AND KEEP YOU STRONG. AND MAY YOU HAVE THE POWER TO UNDERSTAND, AS ALL GOD'S**

PEOPLE SHOULD, HOW WIDE, HOW LONG, HOW HIGH, AND HOW DEEP HIS LOVE IS. MAY YOU EXPERIENCE THE LOVE OF CHRIST, THOUGH IT IS TOO GREAT TO UNDERSTAND FULLY. THEN YOU WILL BE MADE COMPLETE WITH ALL THE FULLNESS OF LIFE AND POWER THAT COMES FROM GOD. (Ephesians 3:14-19 NLT)

Afterword

I am very thankful to Ellie Carman, who has done a thorough job in editing this book and correcting my many mistakes of grammar and punctuation. Thanks as well to Trevor Galpin for writing the Foreword and to Barry Adams for not only his Endorsement, but also his encouragement to write the book and share the reality of our relationship with Father.

Here are details of other resources you may want to look at as you live in the Father's love.

A Father to YOU - www.afathertoyou.com
Audio and video teachings, teaching materials, inspirational videos and details of events in the UK.

The Father's Love Letter - www.fathersloveletter.com
An intimate message from God to you, in over 80 languages.

Fatherheart TV – www.fatherheart.tv
Inspirational videos and live webcasts to inspire and help you grow in the love of the Father.

Fatherheart Ministries – www.fatherheart.net
The ministry of James and Denise Jordan with details of the International schools and other events. Complete with online store with excellent teaching resources.